MW00563357

THE ULTIMATE GUIDE TO
CRYSTAL
GRIDS

Transform Your Life Using the Power of Crystals and Layouts

JUDY HALL

FAIR WINDS

Brimming with creative inspiration, how-to projects, and useful
information to enrich your everyday life, Quarto Knows is a favorite
destination for those pursuing their interests and passions. Visit our
site and dig deeper with our books into your area of interest:
Quarto Creates, Quarto Cooks, Quarto Homes, Quarto Lives,
Quarto Drives, Quarto Explores, Quarto Gifts, or Quarto Kids.

© 2018 Quarto Publishing Group USA Inc.
Text © 2018 Judy Hall

First Published in 2018 by Fair Winds Press, an imprint of The Quarto Group,
100 Cummings Center, Suite 265-D, Beverly, MA 01915, USA.
T (978) 282-9590 F (978) 283-2742 QuartoKnows.com

All rights reserved. No part of this book may be reproduced in any form without written permission of the copyright owners.
All images in this book have been reproduced with the knowledge and prior consent of the artists concerned, and no
responsibility is accepted by producer, publisher, or printer for any infringement of copyright or otherwise, arising from
the contents of this publication. Every effort has been made to ensure that credits accurately comply with information
supplied. We apologize for any inaccuracies that may have occurred and will resolve inaccurate or missing information
in a subsequent reprinting of the book.

Fair Winds Press titles are also available at discount for retail, wholesale, promotional, and bulk purchase. For details, contact
the Special Sales Manager by email at specialsales@quarto.com or by mail at The Quarto Group, Attn: Special Sales Manager,
401 Second Avenue North, Suite 310, Minneapolis, MN 55401, USA.

22 21 20 19 18   1 2 3 4 5

ISBN: 978-1-59233-781-1

Digital edition published in 2018

Library of Congress Cataloging-in-Publication Data available

Design: Samantha J. Bednarek
Cover Image: Michael Illas Photography
Page Layout: Samantha J. Bednarek
Photography: Michael Illas Photography, except pages 85 (bottom two), 145 (top right), 161 (bottom right) by author; page 103
(top right/bottom two) by Jeni Campbell; pages 71, 85 (top two), 89, 93, 97, 103 (top left), 121, 145 (top left/bottom two), 149,
161 (top two/bottom left), 167 by shutterstock.com

Illustration: Holly Neel

No medical claims are made for the crystals in this book and the information given is not intended to act as a substitute for
medical treatment. If in any doubt about their use, a qualified crystal healing practitioner should be consulted. In the context of
this book, illness is a dis-ease, the final manifestation of spiritual, environmental, psychological, karmic, emotional, or mental
imbalance or distress. Healing means bringing mind, body, and spirit back into balance and facilitating evolution for the soul; it
does not imply a cure. In accordance with crystal healing consensus, all stones are referred to as crystals regardless of whether
or not they have a crystalline structure.

DEDICATION

To crystal lovers everywhere

CONTENTS

CRYSTAL POSSIBILITIES

"If you want to find the secrets of the universe, think in terms of energy, frequency, and vibration."—Nikola Tesla

CRYSTAL GRIDS synthesize powerful crystal vibrations and sacred geometric energy. To put it simply, they are energetic technology in action. Each grid has a unique harmonic resonance, and to stand inside a crystal grid is to experience the creative matrix of the universe made manifest. Being in the energy of a grid can be a vibrant event, profoundly energizing and expansive—or it can be a deeply peaceful experience that brings you to a point of stillness and ultimate union. It all depends on the intention of the individual grid.

CRYSTAL GRIDDING

Grids underpin our world. They are found throughout nature: in the perfect spiral of a sunflower or a pinecone; in the precise curves of an ammonite; in the cells of a honeycomb; or in the hidden beauty of a snowflake. They are the internal lattice structure of a crystal—and of the human body. Functioning rather like cosmic glue, grids support the visible and invisible worlds. In Drunvalo Melchizedek's words, they are the "architecture of the universe." And, once you begin to look for them, you'll see them everywhere. Under X-ray defraction, a Beryl crystal, for instance, displays the Flower of Life within its atomic structure. Cut an apple crossways and it reveals a natural pentagram. And the chambered nautilus forms a perfect, progressive spiral. It grows at a constant rate and its shell accommodates that expansion.

"Life itself as we know it is inextricably interwoven with geometric forms, from the angles of atomic bonds in the molecules of the amino acids, to the helical spirals of DNA, to the spherical prototype of the cells, to the first few cells of an organism which assume vesical, tetrahedral, and star (double) tetrahedral forms …" —Bruce Rawles

Crystal grids are potent tools because they harness nature's own manifestation energy. And combining several crystals into a grid has a far greater impact than placing one crystal alone. Whether a grid is created from a single type of crystal or from two or more types, the synergetic interaction of the crystal vibrations with the underlying forcefield, imbued with personal intent, becomes incredibly "power-full."

While a grid seems to be a flat, one-dimensional shape, it actually creates a multi-dimensional energetic net that expands throughout the space in which the grid is situated.

This forcefield amps up your intention exponentially. A small triangular layout, for instance, energetically cleanses and protects a whole house, while a simple spiral radiates energy over a vast area or attracts abundant prosperity into its center. And a hexagram placed on a photograph energetically transfers healing to a person at a distance.

Placing your grid on a cloth or background of a complementary color enhances the power of your grid even further. Use natural base materials whenever possible, such as wood, linen, cotton, slate, or stone, as they will help anchor and actualize the grid's energies (although the color of a cloth is more important than the material from which it's made).

THE PURPOSE OF A GRID

The possibilities for a grid are endless. Grids can be large or small; they can be placed indoors, on or around your body, or in the environment. Remember that a grid's energetic net spreads way beyond the grid itself, so size is not an issue—a small one can be very powerful indeed. And grids offer countless benefits. They can create abundance, safeguard space, and neutralize toxic dross. They can attract love into your life, or send forgiveness and healing intent. They can be set up for world peace, or to heal a devastated forest and the after-effects of a natural disaster.

Grids stabilize and cleanse energies, too, and they're valued for their beneficial effects on the human energy field. Grids unblock and rebalance the chakras and aura, dispersing dis-ease and creating well-being. They can be used for relaxation, emotional clearing, support, or deep healing, or for more specific outcomes, such as overcoming insomnia or headaches, or the detrimental effects of electromagnetic fields. Grids created for a specific outcome such as these can be left in place for long periods, provided that the crystals are regularly cleansed.

> # Crystal Grid
>
> Based on the subtle energy dynamics of sacred geometry, a crystal grid is a precise pattern laid using empowered crystals for the purpose of manifesting a desired outcome, or for cleansing and safeguarding a space.

But there is no hard and fast rule for how long a grid needs to be left in place—or for which grid to choose. Trust yourself. Whichever grid shape appeals to you is the right grid for you. And whatever feels energetically *right* ensures the best outcome for you. Don't hesitate to experiment and modify the shape of a grid to suit your needs if your intuition tells you this would be more beneficial. When a grid has completed its work, thank it and then dismantle it. (Pages 28 to 39 will show you the fundamentals of laying and caring for your grid.)

INTENTION

Clear intention is the key to successful grid-working, as is holding or maintaining that intent as the grid is set out. Intention is what empowers and activates the crystals and fires up the grid. Then, once it's activated, the grid is left to function without interference. But that doesn't mean that you can forget about your grid after you've laid and activated it. It's still important that you remain gently aware of how your intention is progressing over time—without constantly focusing on it or projecting it into the future—and that you cleanse your grid regularly. You'll know if you need to cleanse your grid—or rearrange the crystals or add or subtract appropriate ones—because you'll notice that energy begins to dissipate rather than build each day. (To learn how to cleanse your grid, see page 28.) If this occurs, cleanse your crystals, add or subtract appropriate crystals if necessary, and recharge them with intention. There is no set schedule for doing this. Simply remain aware of your intention, and trust your intuition to tell you when your grid should be cleansed. (After cleansing, you may notice an immediate resurgence of the crystals' energy, or it may rebuild slowly as it shifts to accommodate changes that have already occurred.)

INTUITION

Laying out grids helps you to develop your intuition: the "inner sight" that simply *knows*. Intuition helps you to recognize the appropriate placement for a crystal or exactly the right grid for your purpose, because it tunes into your body's innate, but largely unconscious until developed, ability to read energies. So, the more you rely on your intuition when selecting or using crystals, the stronger your intuition will become. In your crystal work, always go with your heart, the seat of the intuition, rather than your head.

USING THIS BOOK

This book is designed to be a roadmap, a guide to harnessing the phenomenal power of crystals combined with sacred geometry. The more you use it, the more proficient you will become. So, every time you start a new project, lay a grid. Whenever you feel out of sorts, anxious, or ill at ease, lay a grid. If you have a desire to manifest an outcome, create a grid. If you want to protect your space, or to see peace in our world, build a grid. You'll find plenty of examples and grid-kit suggestions to guide you in this book. You can place your own crystals over those in the photographs or lay the grids on backgrounds that are appropriate for you. As you become more familiar with the technique, feel free to adapt the basic grids, or to use the more advanced grids, if you like. And if you come across any unfamiliar terms as you read, check out the glossary on page 182. But whatever you do, activate your grids with focused intention—and then watch the results unfold with awe and thankfulness.

CHAPTER ONE

THE LANGUAGE OF CREATION

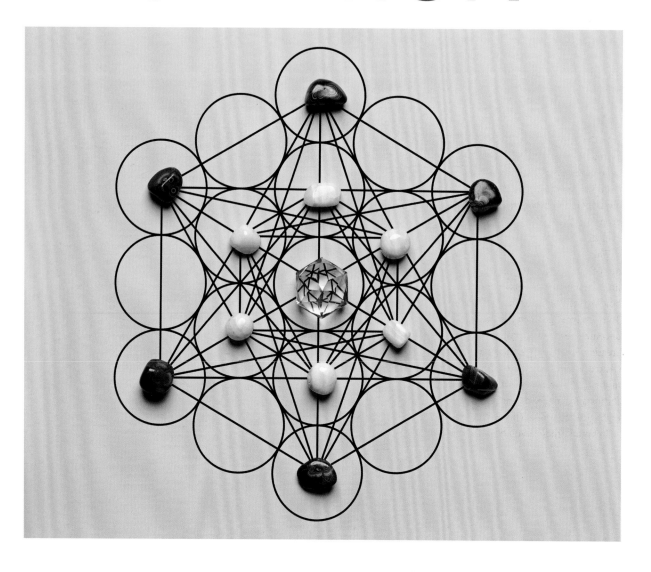

SACRED GEOMETRY: THE BUILDING BLOCKS OF THE UNIVERSE

"Sacred Geometry is the root language, or language of creation, a blueprint of perfection which simply means the intended plan or design. It is a universal language which reminds us of who we were and who we are. Sacred Geometry can assist us in aligning to our true purpose and life path."
—Drunvalo Melchizedek

The orbit of Venus as viewed from Earth

Sacred geometry is the archetypal structure of life—the form in which creation organizes itself, and the foundation on which the entire natural world is built. It could also be called the universal codes, since every natural pattern of growth conforms to one or more geometric shapes. Through sacred geometry we discover the inherent proportion, balance, and harmony that exists in any situation, in all manifest reality, and in everyday life. Sacred geography, the interaction between sacred geometry and matter, describes the fundamental structure of space, time, and everything in between.

This means that sacred geometry is deeply rooted both in our cell memory and in the universe around us. In ancient times, mathematics was at once a sacred science and an art, holding the secrets of the divine and the natural worlds. Today, sacred geometry is the legacy of that knowledge. It encompasses natural proportions that are pleasing to the eye, creating a sense of balance and harmony in the beholder. (And crystal grids harness that power.) It is also described in the cycles and orbits of the planets around us. Venus, for instance, traces a beautiful multi-leaved pattern over an eight-year period when viewed from the perspective of Earth.

Let me introduce you to some of the major designs in sacred geometry.

Unbounderied Flower of Life

Bounderied Flower of Life

FLOWER OF LIFE:
CIRCLES OF THE COSMIC MIND

The Flower of Life is as old as time itself, and is one of the most important examples of sacred geometry. Indeed, it depicts the geometry of both time and space, and encompasses the foundational building blocks of life. The Flower of Life is composed of nineteen overlocking circles of equal radius, with the outer circles arranged around a central circle to create flower-like "petals." The Flower can be infinitely expanded by adding additional overlapping circles radiating out from the center. It is engraved on the pillars of the Osirion at Abydos in Egypt—a structure whose origins are lost in the mists of time, as it way predates the later temple that sits on top of it. Of course, while it's not certain that the design is contemporary with this ancient piece of Egyptian cosmic engineering—the pillars are more than 5,000 years old—it may well be so. As for the engraving itself, the best guess at the moment is that it was made at some point between 500 and 300 BCE. And we do know that the Flower was known to the Greek mathematician Pythagoras (circa 570 to 495 BCE), who trained in Egypt.

All Egyptian temples, as well as Eastern temples, synagogues, and, later, churches, were constructed according to sacred and unchanging divine proportions passed down through the ages. And these proportions were derived from the Flower of Life and the Golden Mean, sometimes known as the Golden Ratio or Golden Section—in other words, from sacred geometry. At its simplest, the Golden Mean is found by dividing a line into two parts so that the longer part divided by the smaller part is also equal to the whole length divided by the longer part. It is symbolized by the Greek letter *phi*. From this simple division, increasingly complex geometric figures, such as the spiral and dodecahedron (a three-dimensional shape with twelve equal five-sided plane faces), can be created.

The Osirion itself was a place of annual rebirth and renewal rites, a monument to Osiris, both the Egyptian lord of the dead and the corn god of fertility. The arrival of the annual Nile flood and the subsequent recession of the waters brought life-giving silt to renew the land.

SHAPES WITHIN THE FLOWER

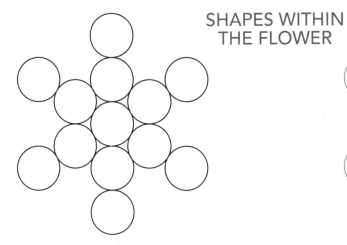

Fruit of Life

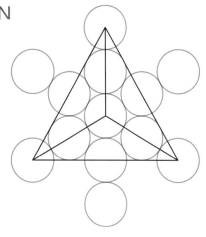

Tetrahedron

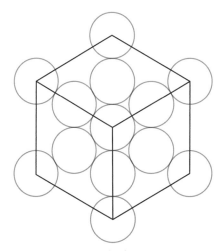

Hexahedron

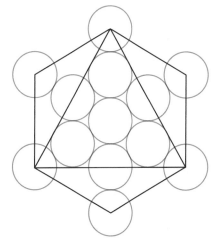

Octahedron

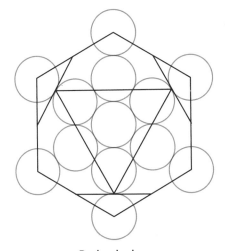

Dodecahedron

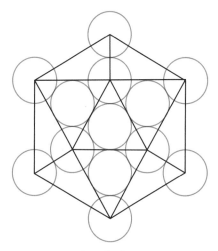

Icosahedron

The Seed of Life (see page 136)

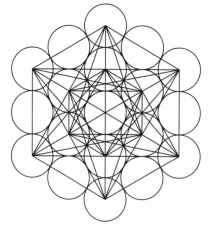

Metatron's Cube (see page 82)

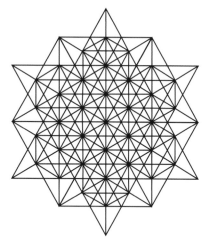

Twelve-pointed star tetrahedron

Merkaba (see page 86)

Despite the construction of the Aswan dam, which was created to block this annual flow, the waters in the Osirion still rise to flood the now-underground chambers at inundation—then recede to allow the hidden columns to rise up, affording access to the heart of the mysteries. This eternal, life-giving cycle is reflected in the unfolding circles of the Flower of Life.

The Flower contains within itself the Seed of Life, the Fruit of Life, the Vesica Piscis, the Tree of Life, the Merkaba, Metatron's Cube, and the Platonic solids. These and other grids are used throughout this book.

The foundational form of the Flower of Life is the circle.

CIRCLE

The circle is pure form without beginning or end. It is the origin of everything. In sacred geometry, it represents unity and completeness. Divide the circle, or replicate it, and you have the beginnings of a grid. The Vesica Piscis (see page 52) is formed from two interlocking circles; from it, all other shapes can be created. In fact, the human eye is a natural Vesica Piscis, through which we perceive the world around us.

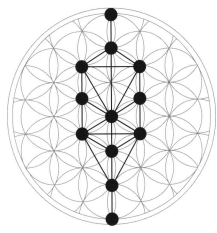

Tree of Life (see page 80)

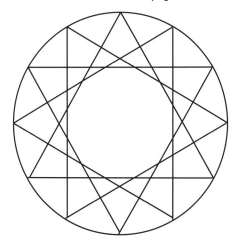

Double Merkaba (see page 90)

The Vesica Piscis also represents feminine energy. When a sperm pierces an ovum and conception occurs, the cell separates first into a Vesica Piscis and then creates a Seed of Life (see page 136).

TRIANGLE

According to the third-century BCE geometer Euclid, the triangle was the first primal shape—although it is constructed within the Vesica Piscis. Indeed, the triangle is the core of the crystal and elemental worlds. An equilateral triangle— that is, a triangle with equal sides and angles—creates five regular polyhedral shapes: the Platonic solids (see page 16), which lock together to form the internal crystal lattices (see page 22). To the ancient Greeks, these shapes symbolized the elements of fire, earth, air, water, and spirit or ether. Another

Basic Guide to Shapes

Virtually all sacred geometry is founded on simple, basic shapes that can be locked together in ever-increasing complexity. A circle is a perimeter, for instance, but becomes a grid when two or more are joined or overlapped. Each shape has a specific purpose and meaning:

- **Circle:** unity, completion, protection, boundary, initiation, healing
- **Triangle:** protection, manifestation, creation, integration
- **Square:** consolidation, stability, strength, protection
- **Spiral:** vortex energy, drawing in, radiating or releasing energy
- **Pyramid:** creation, rebirth, out-of-body journeying
- **Pentagon (five-sided polygon):** stability, clearing, completeness, the elements
- **Pentacle (five-pointed star):** drawing down energy, magical protection, connecting the elements
- **Hexagram (six-pointed star):** protection, energy balancing, consolidation, uniting heart and mind, above and below
- **Sphere:** encompassing all, inherently unstable
- **Cube:** limiting and delineating, inherently stable

Greek geometer, Archimedes, later expanded the five Platonic solids into thirteen complex primal shapes, using isosceles triangles, pentagons, and hexagrams. But it might surprise you to learn that some of these primal shapes had already been identified in Scotland over a thousand years earlier, where they appeared as carved stone "petrospheres." There appears to be nothing new under the sun!

SPIRALS

Spirals are the genesis of life, best demonstrated by the center of a sunflower, the imprint of an ammonite fossil, or the living shell of a nautilus. Spirals are the product of the Golden Mean (more on that in a moment). Their helical shape creates an energetic vortex that spins energy inward or outward, clockwise or counterclockwise. Associated with the omphalos, which is the center point or navel of the Earth, and with natural cycles, they are carved on ancient monuments all over the world. Spirals have an astronomical measuring function, too, including the plotting of the yearly cycles of the sun, moon, and planets.

PLATONIC SOLIDS:
THE BUILDING BLOCKS OF LIFE

The ancient Greeks called the Platonic solids the "five perfect shapes," and believed that they were the core pattern behind physical creation. And in the 1980s, Professor Robert Moon at the University of Chicago demonstrated that the Platonic solids are, in fact, the foundation for the arrangement of protons and neutrons across the entire periodic table of elements. This means that literally everything in the physical universe is based on these five forms, which fits neatly into the ancient Greek assertion that the solids were the four elements that underpinned the physical world, while a fifth element—ether, or life force—animated the whole.

A grid containing one of the fundamental shapes incorporates its specific qualities and elements into the manifestation process. The Platonic solids are:

Octahedron: air, perfect manifestation
Icosahedron: water, expansion, flow
Tetrahedron: fire, creation, destruction, renewal
Cube: Earth, stability
Dodecahedron: spirit/ether, the universe, the divine nature

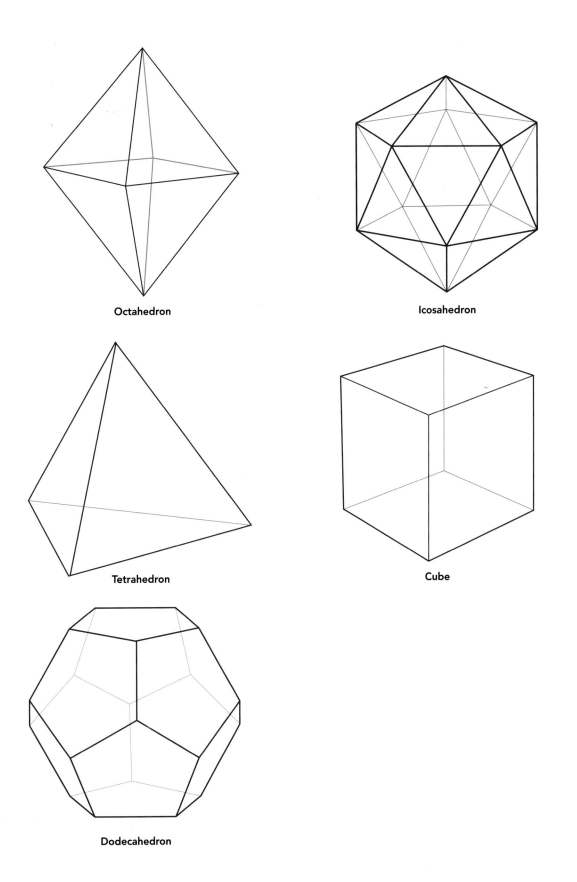

Octahedron

Icosahedron

Tetrahedron

Cube

Dodecahedron

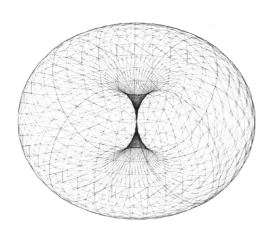

Torus from the side

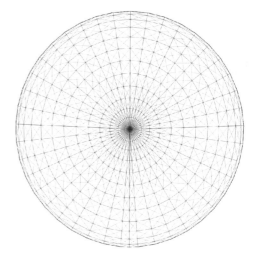

Torus from above

TORUS

The torus is a donut-shaped ring of energy created by an infinite number of circles rotated around a central point. It describes the way in which energy flows out and around a central core. The Earth's magnetic field, for instance, produces a torus. The waves flowing out from the planet are ultimately contained and returned rather than flowing into space, and the result closely resembles Kirlian photography of the energy pattern around a crystal—or, indeed, the human energy field. Energy circulates around a grid in a similar manner, concentrated around the central keystone.

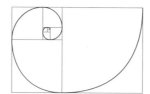

Golden Ratio spiral

THE FIBONACCI SERIES, THE GOLDEN RATIO, AND THE GOLDEN RATIO SPIRAL

In 1202, Leonardo of Pisa, known as Fibonacci, published a book titled *Liber Abaci*, introducing what came to be known as the Fibonacci series to the western world. In the Fibonacci series, the sequence of numbers is generated by adding the previous two numbers together: 1, 2, 3, 5, 8, 13, 21, 34, 55, and so on. When a number in the series is divided into the one following it in the sequence, the result is close to 1.618803 or phi—the Golden Ratio. Known to even the earliest civilizations, the Golden Ratio has been called the fingerprint of creation, because so many buildings and natural formations are founded on it. It creates harmonious, sacred architecture and a template for growth within plants. However, this Golden Ratio produces something much more fundamental to living organisms: deoxyribonucleic acid (DNA). And it also produces the Golden Ratio spiral, the basis for an extremely potent energy management grid (see page 67).

Next, we'll see how a crystal's color and shape express its properties, and how these affect its usage in grids.

NATURE'S PAINTBOX: THE ART OF COLOR

"Look deep into nature, and then you will understand everything better."
—Albert Einstein

Crystals are found in all the colors of the rainbow, and in all the hues of the earth. Some crystals are only one color, others several. When light hits a solid object, such as a crystal, light is refracted into the color spectrum. Color is produced when a portion of that spectrum is absorbed and the remainder reflected. White results from total reflection; black from total absorption. Inclusions and fractures in the crystal lattice also create plays of color, which is also subtly affected by minerals and trace elements within a crystal. But these can be replicated artificially and affect both the "color" that is perceived and the way in which energy moves through the crystal. Our bodies are extremely sensitive to these subtle vibrations of light and color.

NATURAL OR DYED?

Some crystals, such as Quartz, may be naturally amended by ultraviolet rays from the sun, gamma rays from space, or radioactivity from uranium traces, which forms Smoky Quartz. Not all crystal color alteration is natural, however. Crystals may be alchemicalized or heat-treated, color-infused, or dyed. And the effects of these treatments vary. Bright-yellow "Citrine" is often created from heat-treated Amethyst or Smoky Quartz. However, it may lack the dynamic potency of natural Citrine, although it looks bright and works well in a grid. Much of the beautiful violet Tanzanite on sale has been heat-treated to intensify the color, as has bright turquoise Paraiba Tourmaline. Some crystals are color-infused to amp up their properties, and others alchemicalized with precious metals to a whole new vibration. Adding color through dyeing does not add to the crystal's innate properties, although it may make them prettier to look at, as in the case of Howlite and Agate.

(Whether or not you use "treated" crystals like these is a matter of personal taste combined with the intention you've set for your grid. I use a few, such as heat-treated Citrine and some of the more potent alchemical stones, in my grids.)

ALCHEMICAL CRYSTALS

Crystal alchemy is rooted in the age-old search for a method for turning base metals into gold. Sparkling Goldstone, for instance, is created from glass and copper, and it attracts abundance to the user. Aura Quartzes are also alchemically produced. Precious metals such as gold, indium, and titanium are electrostatically bonded onto the surface of Quartz and similar crystals to create a shimmering effect. Such alchemical crystals, which combine the healing properties of the crystal and the metal, can be potent healers and vibration transformers—but crystals that have been dyed or artificially amended to attain the same appearance are not.

THE EFFECT OF COLOR

Color subtly alters the way a crystal functions in a grid. Vibrant "hot" colors energize and stimulate, while paler colors tend to be calming and "cool." Compare the hot pink joy and rejuvenation grid for the environment (see cover and page 165) with exactly the same basic grid laid out in cooling, calming greens around soothing, muted paler pinks to create tranquility within the home (see page 163). Only a handful of the crystals were replaced, but the difference in effect is immediately apparent.

Transparent crystals may be either energizing or dissipating, as required by the individual grid, harmonizing its energetics. Dark colors, on the other hand, transmute and ground energy. Black crystals, such as Smoky Quartz or Shungite, have a structure that captures energy as the light is absorbed. This means that the crystal draws in and holds toxic energies such as electromagnetic "smog," or ill-wishing. They also anchor the grid into the environment.

In modern crystal healing, each color is associated with a chakra and has a specific purpose. (For more on chakras, see page 42.) But this doesn't limit the use of crystals to those color–chakra combinations, especially when applied to grids. During crystal healing and grid work, some areas may need sedating and others may need stimulating. Choosing an appropriate color or colors of crystal harmonizes the energy flow. Color is not the only indicator of how a crystal's energy functions, however. As we will see, shape also plays its part.

CRYSTAL COLOR SPECTRUM

Black: Black crystals are strongly protective. They entrap negative energies that are then either neutralized or transmuted into positive energy. For this reason, they make excellent detoxifiers. They can also help to identify gifts that are hidden in the shadows—that is, they can help you to recognize potential and opportunities that you may not have been aware of before. Grids from black crystals ground the physical body and protect the environment.

Brown: Brown crystals resonate with the earth chakras. They are cleansing and purifying, grounding and protective. Use them to absorb toxic emanations and negative energies, and to induce stability and centeredness. They are excellent for long-term use but need regular cleansing.

Silver-Gray: Metallic and silvery-gray crystals have alchemical properties of transmutation. That is, they convert negative energy into positive. They make excellent journeying crystals, traditionally imparting invisibility, helping the traveler to pass safely and unharmed. These crystals resonate with the earth chakras and are useful for shadow work. The shadow is a disowned, dejected, rejected, and isolated part of the overall Self that tends to be denied, and so it gets projected "out there" into external experiences. It forms an unconscious snag, thwarting our most well-meant intentions. Home to the wounds left over from ancestral trauma, childhood, and previous lives, it also contains gifts that have been repressed. As crystals heal the energetic patterns that contain the wounds, it is not always necessary to connect to their source. Integrating the shadow through journeying, crystal work, or therapy opens up a new emotional vitality.

Gold: Gold stones have long been associated with abundance and manifestation, as they generate energy and also facilitate en*lighten*ment. Use them for long-term grids to draw prosperity and new vitality into your life.

Red: Red crystals resonate with the base and sacral chakras. They energize and activate, strengthening libido and stimulating creativity. Red crystals generate and circulate energy as required. This effect can be extremely stimulating, though, and may over-excite volatile emotions, so red crystals are best for short-term use.

Pink: Exceedingly gentle, pink crystals carry the essence of unconditional love and promote forgiveness. In grids, they attract more love into the seeker's life. They can provide comfort and alleviate anxiety, making them useful "first-aid" emotional heart-healers. Pink crystals also help to overcome loss, release grief, and dispel trauma. Instilling acceptance, they resonate with the three-chambered heart chakra and are ideal for long-term use.

Peach: Gently energizing peach crystals unite the heart and sacral chakras, combining love with action. Use them in grids intended to help you move forward placidly in your life.

Orange: Orange crystals activate and release, and are useful for building up energetic structures, since their energetic output locks together and does not dissipate. Many attract abundance, and, with vibrant vitality, they stimulate creativity and increase assertiveness. An orange grid grounds projects into the physical world and gets things done. This color resonates with the sacral chakra.

Yellow: Yellow crystals work with the solar plexus and the mind, balancing emotion and intellect; a yellow grid instills clarity. They're excellent for reducing seasonal depression, bringing the warmth of the sun into winter.

Green: Calming and cleansing, green crystals resonate with the heart chakra, providing emotional healing and instilling compassion and tranquility. They also draw higher consciousness down to Earth, anchoring it. A green grid is useful when energy needs sedating or when emotions need pacifying.

Green-Blue and turquoise: These crystals resonate with higher levels of being, stimulating spiritual awareness and metaphysical abilities. Many turquoise crystals connect to cosmic consciousness, drawing it down to Earth, and all instill profound peace and relaxation. These crystals work at the third eye and soma chakras, uniting the heart and intuition.

Blue: Blue crystals resonate with the throat, third eye, soma, and causal vortex chakras, stimulating self-expression, facilitating communication, and linking to the highest states of consciousness. They ground or project spiritual energy and assist intuition and channeling. Traditionally, these crystals procured the assistance of spirits of light to counteract darkness. A blue grid stimulates intuition and metaphysical abilities, bringing about mystical perception.

Indigo: Indigo crystals link to the highest states of consciousness and to the most profound depths of space. With powerful spiritual awakening qualities, these crystals integrate and align, stimulating service to others. They can be useful for cooling over-heated energies, too. Stimulating intuition and metaphysical abilities, they bring about mystical perception of the world when placed at the third eye or soma chakras.

Lavender, lilac, and purple: Purple crystals resonate with the higher crown chakras and multi-dimensional realities, drawing spiritual energy into the physical plane, and encouraging service to others. Lavender and violet crystals have a lighter and finer vibration that links to the highest states of awareness.

Magenta: Magenta crystals link to the higher crown chakras, particularly the soul star and causal vortex, and stimulate connection to multi-dimensional realities. Use them to open the higher vibration chakras around the head to expand conscious awareness.

Clear or white: Clear crystals carry the vibration of pure light and higher consciousness. They resonate with the higher crown chakras. These crystals purify and focus energy, linking to the highest realms of being. Use them when situations need clarifying, or for opening intuition and gaining insight. Clear crystals are powerful energizers, radiating energy into the environment. In grids, they purify and heal the aura and physical body.

Combination and bi-colored crystals: Combination crystals create additional possibilities. Synergizing the qualities of component colors or crystals to work holistically together, they are often more effective than individual crystals, because their vibrations are raised to a higher energetic frequency.

NATURE'S TOOL KIT: THE SCIENCE OF SHAPE

"It is structure that we look for whenever we try to understand anything. All science is built upon this search; we investigate how the cell is built of reticular material, cytoplasm, chromosomes; how crystals aggregate; how atoms are fastened together; how electrons constitute a chemical bond between atoms." —Linus Pauling

Crystal shape takes two forms: internal and external. Both affect how energy moves through a grid. First of all, the internal geometric lattice of a crystal defines the system to which it belongs. This lattice, with its precise replication of internal facets and angles, remains the same, regardless of the crystal's external shape. It is found in the even tiniest piece, and it is replicated in the largest. This is why a crystal can be tumbled, raw or faceted, flawless or chipped, small or large, and it still has the same effect—as indeed it does when it takes on apparently very different external forms. To the naked eye, for instance, the brown "sputnik" form of Aragonite has no outward connection with its delicate pink, layered blue, or spiky white relations. But they are classified as the same crystal because their component minerals and internal crystal lattice match exactly. A handful of crystals do not have an internal lattice, such as Obsidian, which formed rapidly, or Amber, a natural solidified resin. Energy flows smoothly through non-crystalline structures like these, since there are no impediments to affect its passage, but it can also "suck out" blockages and distortions as there is no specific direction of flow.

A crystal's external shape, whether natural or achieved by cutting and polishing, doesn't affect its inherent properties; but, as we'll see later on in this chapter, it does mediate how and where crystal energy flows.

UNIVERSAL BUILDING BLOCKS

The ancient Greek mathematician Pythagoras (whose father was a gem-cutter in Egypt) recognized that the universe is made up of a mere handful of geometric shapes. These shapes are the fundamental components of virtually all crystal grids. However, crystals themselves reflect these universal building blocks, too. At the heart of a crystal is its stable lattice. Within this structure, dynamic particles rotate in constant motion around a central point, generating energy. So, although a crystal may look outwardly serene, it is actually a seething molecular mass vibrating at a specific frequency—and generating energy. As the crystal frequency is stable and "pure," crystals entrain—that is, bring into balance—energy fields around them, which makes them extremely effective stabilizers. In this way, grids transform unstable energy patterns, such as the human body or its environment.

THE CRYSTAL SYSTEMS

Crystals are created from atoms that are packed together in an orderly fashion: the internal lattice. And individual crystals are recognizable by the way in which their component molecules fill the internal space. Each family of crystals has its own unique signature or crystal lattice. Under a microscope, a large, small, or differently colored example of the same crystal has exactly the same lattice. It will, however, also belong to an overall crystal group, or "family." Each crystal system functions in a slightly different way, channeling energy according to the lattice. There are seven main crystal groups, plus the amorphous system, which has no lattice. (Solidified natural substances, such as Amber, are deemed amorphous.) The crystal systems are:

Amorphous or organic (no lattice): Energy flows rapidly and can be a catalyst for growth, or can induce a cathartic release of toxicity. Amorphous energy surrounds and protects a body or a space.

Isometric (cubic): Stabilizes, grounds, and cleanses energy; releases tension and encourages creativity. Cubic crystals are excellent for grids that create structure and reorganization. This is the only crystal form that does not bend rays of light as they pass through it.

Hexagonal: Organizes and balances energy and provides support; useful for exploring specific issues.

Monoclinic: Increases perception and balances the systems of the body; useful for purification.

Orthorhombic: Vibrant and energetic; cleanses and dispels, increases the flow of information.

Tetragonal: Transformational. Opens, harmonizes, and balances energy flow, and brings resolution.

Triclinic: Protective, integrating energy and opposites; opens perception, facilitating exploration of other dimensions.

Trigonal (hexagonal): Focuses and anchors energy, invigorates, and protects the aura and environment.

THE EFFECT OF EXTERNAL SHAPE

Although the internal lattice—which is not visible to the naked eye—is fundamental to crystal energy, external shape has a bearing, too. The outer form of a crystal, especially when it's artificially shaped, does not necessarily reflect its inner lattice, but it may subtly amend the way in which energy flows through it.

Ball: Emits energy equally all round. Forms a window to facilitate movement through time. Balls make an excellent centerpiece for a grid that radiates energy into the environment.

Cluster: Several points on a base radiate energy multidirectionally. These make a useful keystone for grids.

Double terminated: Points at both ends emit energy. Double terminations break old patterns and move energy in both directions through a grid.

Egg: Gently pointed end focuses energy. Rounded end radiates it more widely. Place point-down in a grid to channel energy into a body or the earth, or place point-up to radiate it out.

Elestial: Folded with many terminations, windows, and inner planes, an elestial radiates gently flowing energy that opens the way to insight and change. These make a useful keystone or anchor for grids.

Faceted: Semi-precious and precious stones are often faceted to increase the amount of light penetrating the crystal, creating brilliance. This does not make them more effective for use in a grid: raw or tumbled stones work just as well.

Generator: Six-pointed end or several points radiating equally in all directions. Focuses healing energy or intention, draws people together.

Geode: Hollow "cave"-like formation amplifies, conserves, and slowly releases energy. Geodes are useful when energy is stagnant and needs constant, steady revitalization. They are also helpful where earth energy is flowing too fast and the grid has been placed to slow or redirect the flow.

Manifestation: A smaller crystal encased within an outer crystal. As its name suggests, it carries the power of manifestation, especially of abundance, but can be harnessed to any intention. Place a manifestation crystal as the keystone in an abundance grid.

Merkaba: A representation of divine "source" energy, a Merkeba is a star tetrahedron, a three-dimensional eight-pointed star created from two triangular pyramids, one pointing up, the other down. It balances and harmonizes energy, stepping down cosmic vibrations and grounding them into the physical plane, uniting "above" with "below." It is the perfect shape for a keystone within a grid as it contains the potential for limitless creation and DNA healing.

Palmstone: Flat and rounded, palmstones calm and soothe the mind. They serve as the perfect keystone for the center of a grid to create what you most desire.

Phantom: Pointed inner pyramid breaks old patterns and raises vibrations. Place phantoms point-out in an environmental grid to break old patterns, and point inward in a grid placed on a body for the same purpose.

Point: Naturally faced point draws off energy when pointed out from the body, and draws energy in when pointed toward the body. Useful for cleansing and energizing a grid.

Pyramid: A pyramidal crystal creates energy and fountains it out from its point. Or, it can protect internal space. Pyramids make excellent keystones in grids.

Raw: A rough chunk of the natural crystal or stone. Works well in grids, since the artificial shaping of crystals can subtly amend the natural energetic flow of the crystal material. Raw chunks are also ideal for outdoor grids, as they do not scratch and can withstand the weather.

Scepter: A crystal formed around a central core rod is an excellent tool for inputting power and restructuring. It activates a grid.

Square: Consolidating energy, a square grounds and anchors intention. Naturally occurring square crystals such as Pyrite draw off negative energy and transform it.

Tumbled: Gently rounded stones draw off negative energy, or bring in positive energy. They are ideal for use in grids as they do not have to be direction-specific.

Wand: Long-pointed, or specially shaped crystals focus energy and draw it off, or bring in energy, depending on which way the point is facing. Useful for joining crystals in a grid to activate the energetic net.

CHAPTER TWO

PREPARING AND SETTING UP A GRID

FINDING EXACTLY the right combination of crystals for your grid is the key to crystal power. While I offer suggestions in the grid-kits throughout this book, there's no need to feel limited by these suggestions. Use whichever crystals feel appropriate. You may well have crystals in your collection that would be perfect for your intention. (If you need to know the properties of specific crystals, you'll find a list of appropriate reference books in the Resources section on page 184.) This chapter will guide you to choose the right crystals to match your intention, and will lay out the basic guidelines for setting up a grid. Finally, it will show you how to care for your crystals both before and after using them in a grid.

CRYSTAL SELECTION

When you're choosing a crystal, remember that biggest and flashiest isn't necessarily the best, especially for crystal grids. It's not the outward beauty of a crystal that dictates its power; it's the crystal's individual properties. A rough lump of raw rock may be more powerful than an expensively presented gemstone, no matter how seductive the latter may be. Crystals don't have to be "perfect" in terms of their appearance, either. In fact, chips or slight differences in size and shape may make crystals work harder, because they empathize with the knocks and bumps of everyday life. As long as they fit into a grid at an energetic level, such "imperfections" will not distort the underlying geometry.

Choosing slightly different colors or types of crystal can dramatically affect the output of a grid. The grid on the cover of this book, for instance, is laid in exactly the same way as the Sphere of Tranquility (see Specific Grids, pages 163 to 165). But, due to color enhancement to the hot pink crystals, it is a grid of vibrant joy and rejuvenation rather than calm serenity. The joy grid uses color-coated crystals to powerful effect, although this type of crystal should be selected with care as coating in this way may dull down rather than enhance the energies of an underlying crystal.

You'll probably start by searching out crystals for the purpose for which you are setting up your grid (the grid-kit suggestions will assist you with this). A particular photograph in this book may have caught your attention. If so, that's a good starting point. But where do you go from there—and what if you have no idea which crystals are appropriate for you, right now? Put out the focused thought, "I find exactly the right crystals for me, now." Then run your fingers through a basket of crystals or pass your hand over the tubs that hold tumbled stones. There'll be several that "stick" to your fingers—or the shapes and energy of some crystals will just feel right. That's the intuitive approach. The kinesthetic intuitive approach is to dowse (see page 31) as your body–mind already knows the answer and is waiting to communicate with you.

If you prefer a reasoned, logical approach to an intuitive one, you could peruse the information on how colors, shapes, and specific grids mold the crystals' energy. Check out crystal reference books (see Resources, page 184) and seek crystals to exactly match your intention.

When you've found a crystal, take a few moments to become attuned to it. Hold it in your hands and feel its vibrations radiating into your core being. If those vibrations accord with your own, you feel calm and peaceful. If they are not, you begin to feel nauseous or jittery. If that's the case, you could choose another crystal, as the one you are holding may not be right for you at this time. This may also be an indication of inner work that you need to do, in which case scan through the personal grids (see pages 112 to 161) to see which one jumps out at you as most appropriate at this time.

If your crystal has a pointed termination, face it in the direction in which the energy flows around the grid. Pointing a crystal inward draws in energy; pointing it out draws it off.

Wherever you find your crystals, make sure you cleanse and empower them before use.

Empathy Nicks and Self-Healed Crystals

Crystals for use in grids do not have to be perfect. In fact, points that are chipped or crystals that appear misshapen may work extra hard, as they empathize with wounds and pain and will apply their compassionate healing properties in the grid. "Self-healed" crystals exhibit internal breaks that have healed over time as the crystal continued to grow. Such crystals are particularly useful in healing grids.

CRYSTAL CARE

Crystals constantly pick up energy, in addition to radiating it out. This is especially so when grids are left in place for a long period of time. That means your crystals need regular cleansing. Always start your grid with "clean" crystals and keep the grid cleansed and recharged during its operation. Otherwise, the grid begins to beam detrimental, rather than beneficial, energy as it slowly runs out of steam, especially when it has been transmuting negative energies.

How often you cleanse your crystals depends on the purpose of the grid and on the intensity of the energy being absorbed or radiated. For example, protective and clearing grids need cleansing more frequently than those that attract abundance, love, and so on. Ultimately, there is no set rule as to timing, except to cleanse frequently, and to most definitely cleanse and recharge whenever the crystals begin to look "dull" and the grid is no longer working. Simply placing your hand over the grid will tell you whether the energy is bright and active or sluggish and in need of a reboot. Crystals also require purifying when the grid is dismantled. (To learn how to do this see page 39, and to make a grid-clearing-and-recharging essence, see opposite.)

BEFORE YOU LAY YOUR GRID: INITIAL CRYSTAL CLEANSING

TIP:
To smudge a crystal, hold it in the smoke from an incense stick or smudge bundle for a few moments, ensuring that all sides receive the smoke.

"The sound created by a Tibetan or singing bowl, tingshaws, a gong, or tuning fork is a pure vibration that cleanses and restores all crystals. If using a bowl, several crystals can be put in at once, enough to cover the bottom but not restrict the vibration. Tingshaws and a gong can be struck over several whilst a tuning fork can be struck and applied individually. Whatever you are using, listen carefully, and you will hear when the cleaning and charging is complete, as the sound will be clear and bright." —Terrie Celest, www.astrologywise.co.uk

If the crystals are robust—that is, unless they are layered, fragile, soluble, or have tiny crystals on a matrix—cleanse them in running water, then place them in the sun or moonlight to recharge. If they are less robust, place them in brown rice overnight, smudge them with sweetgrass or incense, or use a singing bowl or tingshaws (see quote above). Then place them in the sun or on a crystal to recharge. If the grid is to be buried in the ground, soak the keystone in Petaltone Z14 (see Resources, page 184) essence before covering, as the clearing effect lasts for several months. Otherwise, leave one crystal above the ground so that it can be sprayed regularly.

Once your grid is in place, lightly spray it with crystal clearing and recharge essence weekly (see opposite), or whenever the energy feels depleted or stagnant.

RECHARGING YOUR CRYSTALS

Place a crystal in the sun or moonlight for a few hours to recharge it or spray it with recharging essence. Placing crystals on large energizing crystals such as Carnelian or Quartz will also recharge your grids. (You may need to remove the crystals for a short time in order to do this.) If the grid is to be buried, leave one of the stones poking above ground to receive the sun's rays. Or spray with a recharging essence once cleansed (see Resources, page 184).

GRID CLEARING AND RECHARGE ESSENCE

Ready-made crystal clearing essence sprays cleanse crystals and are especially useful for a grid that remains in place (see Resources, page 184), as you don't need to move the crystals to cleanse them. You can also make your own cleansing and recharge spray. This essence also closes down the space after a grid has been deactivated and the crystals removed, which is not usually a function of ready-made sprays.

CRYSTAL CLEANSING AND RECHARGE SPRAY

To make your own crystal cleansing and recharge spray, you will need:

CLEARING

- Black Tourmaline
- Blue or Black Kyanite
- Hematite
- Shungite
- Smoky Quartz

RECHARGING

- Anandalite™
- Carnelian
- Golden Healer Quartz
- Citrine
- Orange Kyanite
- Quartz
- Red Jasper
- Selenite (use tumbled)

TOOLS

- Small glass bowl
- Spring water
- Small glass bottle
- Funnel
- Spray bottle
- Frankincense, lavender, sage, or a similar essential oil
- Vodka or white rum

DIRECTIONS

1. Select one or two crystals from the clearing list and one or two from the recharging list on the left. Ensure that the crystals are thoroughly cleansed.
2. Hold them in your hands for a few moments and ask them to cleanse the grid, your crystals, or your space.
3. Place the crystals in a small glass bowl and cover with spring water. (Use fresh water from a pure source; avoid tap water or only use it when nothing else is available. If you do use tap water, include raw Shungite in the crystal mix.)
4. Place the bowl in sunlight for a few hours. Cover if necessary.
5. Remove the crystals and, using a funnel, pour the water into a glass bottle. Fill it one-third full.
6. Add a few drops of essential oil, such as frankincense, sage, or lavender, and top up the bottle with vodka or white rum, which will act as a preservative. This is the mother essence.
7. Label the bottle with the date and contents. You can use it immediately or store it in a cool place for several months.
8. Fill the spray bottle with spring water. Add 7 drops of the mother essence. Label it.
9. Spray the grid from above, lightly misting all the crystals.

SETTING UP YOUR GRID

BASIC GRID-KIT

If you have a few basic cleansed gridding crystals on hand, you can set up a grid instantly. Choose six equal-sized crystals, or as many as the grid requires, and a larger one for the key-stone. A varied selection of crystals is best, but don't overdo the number—three or four types are probably enough. Choose the ones that resonate with you from the following list.

Grounding and anchoring: Boji Stones, Flint, Granite, Hematite, Obsidian, Petrified Wood, Smoky Quartz, Brown Carnelian, Polychrome Jasper, Mookaite Jasper, Picture Jasper

Protective: Amber, Amethyst, Apache Tear, Black Tourmaline, Green Aventurine, Herkimer Diamond, Labradorite, Lepidolite, Shungite, Smoky Quartz, Mookaite Jasper, Porcelain Jasper

Cleansing: Amethyst, Apache Tear, Calcite, Chlorite Quartz, Flint, Halite, Obsidian, Quartz, Selenite, Shungite, Smoky Quartz

Energizing: Carnelian, Citrine, Herkimer Diamond, Lemurian Seed, Quartz, Red Jasper, Imperial Topaz, Sunstone, Ruby, Garnet

Abundance: Carnelian, Citrine, Goldstone, Jade, Tiger's Eye, Topaz

Personal healing: Bloodstone, Quantum Quattro Silica, Que Sera (Llanoite/Vulcanite), Emerald, Shungite, Golden Healer

Environmental healing: Aragonite, Kambaba Jasper, Petrified Wood, Rhodozite, Rose Quartz, Shungite, Smoky Quartz

High-vibration, light-bringing: Anandalite™ (Aurora Quartz), Celtic Quartz, Lemurian Seed, Moldavite, Petalite, Phenacite, Selenite, Trigonic Quartz

Intuitive: Apophyllite, Azurite, Bytownite, Herkimer Diamond, Blue or Green Kyanite, Labradorite, Lapis Lazuli, Larimar, Clear Quartz, Rhomboid Selenite, Selenite, Tangerine Aura Quartz

DOES SIZE MATTER?

It most emphatically does not. Again, when it comes to crystals, the biggest and most beautiful does not equal the most powerful. And while it makes sense to place large crystals where they can be seen if they are to be left in situ, so that they remain undisturbed, smaller or rough pieces work equally well in grids. That's because all crystals of a specific type are connected by what Michael Eastwood, an English crystal authority, calls "the crystal oversouls," which is a unified field of consciousness that interconnects the individual crystals of that type, wherever they may be. The smaller ones take their power from the whole. If you wish, you can place smaller crystals on a larger one of the same type before use to boost their connection to the oversoul power, but this is by no means essential.

DOWSING FOR YOUR CRYSTALS

Dowsing is an easily learned skill that assists not only in selecting crystals, but also in choosing the appropriate grid for your purpose, and in figuring out where to position it. You can use a pendulum or finger dowse (see page 32), whichever you prefer. Neither method is "better" than the other. It is a matter of personal preference and finding which works for you. Each method accesses the ability of your intuitive body–mind connection to tune into subtle vibrations and to influence your hands. A focused mind, trust in the process, and clear, unambiguous intent supports your dowsing.

> You can buy a pendulum at any crystal or New Age shop, or on the Internet. If you prefer, you can also use your fingers to dowse (see page 32).

PENDULUM DOWSING

If you are familiar with pendulum dowsing, use the pendulum in your usual way. If you are not familiar with it, pendulum dowsing is an easy skill to learn. It will assist in placing crystals within a grid, positioning the grid itself, and in establishing how long to leave a grid in place or whether it needs amending from time to time. Pendulum dowsing is particularly useful when placing large outdoor grids or crystals on maps.

To pendulum dowse

1. Hold your pendulum between the thumb and forefinger of your most receptive hand with about a hand's length of chain hanging down to the pendulum. You'll soon recognize a length that's comfortable for you.
2. Wrap the remaining chain around your fingers so that it does not obstruct the dowsing. Tuck your arm into your side, bend your elbow, and hold out your hand at a right angle to your upper arm.
3. Ascertain your "yes" and "no" responses. Some people find that the pendulum swings in one direction for "yes" and at right angles to that axis for "no," while others have a backward and forward swing for one reply, and a circular motion for the other.
4. A "wobble" of the pendulum indicates "maybe," or that it is not appropriate to dowse at that time. In that case, ask whether or not dowsing is appropriate, and if the answer is "yes," check that you are asking the right question. If the pendulum stops completely, this indicates that it is inappropriate to ask at that time.
5. Ascertain your particular pendulum response by holding the pendulum over your knee and asking, "Is my name [give your correct name]?" The direction that the pendulum swings indicates "yes." Check by asking, "Is my name [give incorrect name]?" to establish "no." Or, program in "yes" and "no" by swinging the pendulum in a particular direction a few times, saying as you do so: "This is 'yes'," and swinging it in a different direction to program "no."

To pendulum dowse the best crystal for you

Hold the pendulum in your most receptive hand. Slowly run your finger along the list of possible crystals in the grid-kit suggestions, noting whether you get a "yes" or "no" response. You could also dowse over the illustrations throughout this book, in other crystal books (see Resources, page 184), or in a crystal shop. Check the whole kit to see which "yes" response is strongest, as there may well be several that could be appropriate, or you may need to use several crystals in combination. Another way to do this, if you have a selection of crystals available, is to touch each crystal in turn, again noting the "yes" or "no" response that results.

Exactly where do I place the crystals?

Your pendulum can pinpoint the exact placement for a crystal, which is especially useful when creating large outdoor grids. However, there may be times when a crystal displays a mind of its own and constantly shifts its position slightly out of alignment within the grid. If this is the case, allow the crystal to settle itself, which will open up a space for new possibilities to unfold.

How long should I leave a grid in place?

A pendulum can also be used to establish how long you should leave a grid in place. Some grids may only need to be left in place for a minute or two before being dismantled or re-arranged with fresh crystals. First, ask whether the period required is minutes, hours, days, weeks, or months. When you have ascertained the answer, ask, "One minute [or hour, day, week, or month]? Two minutes [or hours, days, weeks, or months]?" and so on, until the length of time has been ascertained.

FINGER DOWSING

Finger dowsing answers "yes" and "no" questions quickly and unambiguously, and it can be done unobtrusively in situations in which a using pendulum might provoke unwanted attention. This method of dowsing works particularly well for people who are kinesthetic—that is, whose bodies respond intuitively to subtle feelings—but anyone can learn to finger dowse.

To finger dowse

1. Hold the thumb and first finger of your right hand together.
2. Then loop the thumb and finger of your left hand through the first "loop" to make a "chain."
3. Ask clearly and unambiguously whether this is the best and most appropriate crystal for your purpose. Either speak it aloud, or say it within your mind.
4. Now pull gently but firmly. If the chain breaks, the answer is "no." If it holds, the answer is "yes."

To finger dowse timing

Asking about periods of time requires a slightly different method of finger dowsing. First, ask whether the period required is minutes, hours, days, weeks, or months. When you have ascertained the answer, slot your fingers together and ask that they hold until the right answer is reached, then release. Then ask, "One minute [or hour, day, week, or month]? Two minutes [or hours, days, weeks, or months]?" and so on, until the length of time has been ascertained.

EMPOWERING YOUR CRYSTALS WITH INTENTION

To activate your crystals and imbue them with intention, simply hold the cleansed crystals in your hands, focus your attention on them, and say aloud:

I dedicate these crystals to the highest good of all and ask that their power be activated now to work in harmony with my focused intention. I also ask that the grid when assembled will [add your specific purpose for the grid], together with anything else that is appropriate at the highest level.

Remember to restate your intention when you lay the grid.

CHOOSING A LOCATION

The location for your grid needs to be appropriate for your intention and for the period for which the grid is to remain in place. Grids on or around your body are limited, although a grid can be placed around or under a bed, and the energetic effect will continue as a result. Small grids can be left in place in the home or workplace. Bigger grids, which may be placed around a building or in the environment, for instance, can also be left in place as long as they will not be disturbed and are accessible for cleansing. You could also place a grid in your home according to the feng shui bagua (see page 34). Choose a position appropriate to the space that will not be disturbed.

Grids can be placed in the following locations:

On or around your body
In your home or workspace
In the environment
Buried in the ground
On a photograph
On a map

HEALING CHALLENGE

When you're working with grids, a healing challenge—a period of time during which symptoms or situations initially worsen—may occasionally occur. If this happens while you're laying out or lying within a grid, remove yourself and hold detoxifying and restabilizing crystals such as Black Tourmaline, Shungite, Smoky Quartz, Flint, or Hematite. Place one at your feet until the situation settles. Before re-entering or returning to laying the grid, check by dowsing or intuition whether any crystals need to be removed or replaced. When you re-enter the grid, place a grounding and detoxifying crystal at your feet. If the grid has been laid in the environment—including a small grid laid in a room in your house—create a circle around it with the same crystals, or temporarily replace the keystone or anchor crystals with a detoxifying crystal. When the situation has settled, check that the correct crystals are in place, and replace any that have completed their work.

FENG SHUI BAGUA

In feng shui, each area of a house or a room corresponds to an area of life. The easiest map to follow is the one based on the front door or entranceway, located at the bottom center of the map (that is, in career). For example, if your intention were to attract more love into your life, you'd lay a grid in the area of your house that represents relationships or marriage, which is always at the far back right of your house as you face into it from the front door.

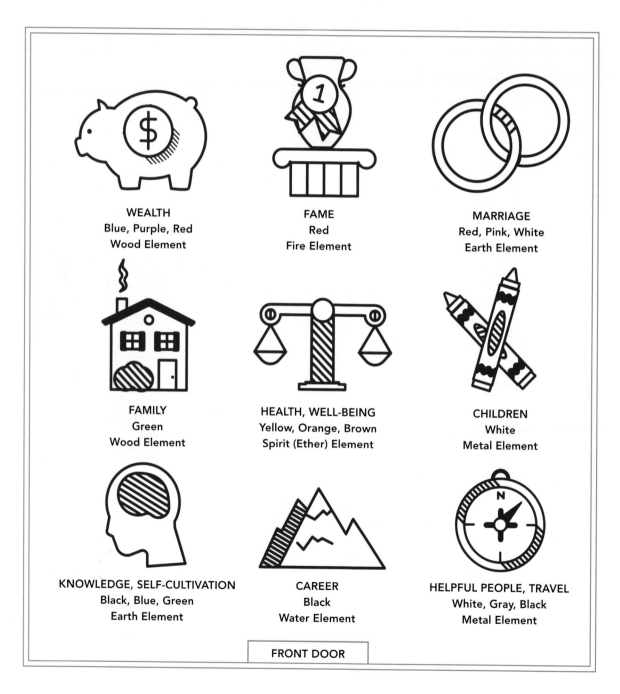

WEALTH
Blue, Purple, Red
Wood Element

FAME
Red
Fire Element

MARRIAGE
Red, Pink, White
Earth Element

FAMILY
Green
Wood Element

HEALTH, WELL-BEING
Yellow, Orange, Brown
Spirit (Ether) Element

CHILDREN
White
Metal Element

KNOWLEDGE, SELF-CULTIVATION
Black, Blue, Green
Earth Element

CAREER
Black
Water Element

HELPFUL PEOPLE, TRAVEL
White, Gray, Black
Metal Element

FRONT DOOR

CHOOSING A GRID TEMPLATE

Match the shape of the grid to your intention and to the space available. If you are a beginner, start with one of the basic shapes, or try an example grid for a specific purpose. As you become familiar with grid energy, choose one of the more complex shapes, or create your own. Don't hesitate to amend or expand a grid that appeals to you. As you will see, some of the specific grids later in this book use variations of a basic template. But, remember that grids do not have to be complicated to be effective.

ALIGNING A GRID

Aligning your grid with the magnetic points of the compass draws in the power of the directions to assist in the work. Aligning a grid north to south smooths the energy flow, for instance, but you can also align it to sun- or moonrise, which varies throughout the year. Sun-orientated grids are active and initiating, while moon-orientated grids are nurturing and initiatory. It is also possible to align your grids in accordance with the traditional associations of the shamanic directions as follows:

North: Knowledge, restructuring, calming discord
South: Cleansing, flowing, and activating
East: Conception, removes strife, motivates new projects
West: Letting go, clearing, growth, renewal, rebirth
Above: Cosmic energy and light, energizing, the divine masculine
Below: Earthing, grounding, nurturing, the divine feminine

THE KEYSTONE: POWERING THE GRID

A point of power, a keystone focuses and amplifies the grid. It is usually the central stone, symbolizing the source of life. The keystone channels universal life force (Qi) to the grid, and its energy is then amplified by the grid. Quartz in its various forms is an ideal keystone, as it constantly transmutes, generates, amplifies, and radiates energy.

HE ANCHORS: STABILIZING THE GRID

Anchor stones hold the energy of a grid in place, grounding and centering it. They may be sited at, or outside, the corners of a square grid, for instance, or within the grid structure itself. Stones such as Flint, Aragonite, Smoky Quartz, or Granite make excellent anchor stones. Flint, Black Tourmaline and Shungite anchor a cleansing or high-vibration crystal grid, channeling transmuted energy down through the multi-dimensions to Earth itself.

THE PERIMETER

A perimeter keeps the energies of a grid free from interference or disruption. It is not necessarily an integral part of the grid itself—although in some cases, it may be. (Perimeters may be important for a grid that's intended to contain energy and create a boundary, such as protecting a space; clearing electromagnetic fields [EMFs] in a house; creating a safe space; or inviting in a higher presence.) Quartz, in one of its many forms, is an ideal perimeter, as is Black Tourmaline or Shungite, since all of these ground the grid into everyday reality. Triclinic crystals, such as Kyanite or Labradorite, or orthorhombic crystals such as Aragonite, also make useful boundary stones, while Selenite creates a protective perimeter of light.

LAYING A GRID

1. Select your location (see page 33).
2. Choose a place and time where and when you will not be disturbed.
3. Cleanse the space on which your grid will be laid (see page 28).
4. Choose an appropriate background and color on which to lay your grid (suggestions are given in each grid).
5. Gather your crystals together and thoroughly cleanse them.
6. Hold them in your hands and state your intention for the grid. Be specific and precise. You might say, "Please protect me and my space," for example.
7. Mark your template or use the examples in this book as a guide. Remember to orient the grid appropriately (see page 35).
8. If your grid is intended to draw energy in or to provide protection, place the outermost crystals first. If your grid is intended to radiate energy, place the keystone first.
9. Check that the crystals are properly aligned. But note that if a crystal continually shifts its position, this may be to open up the unrecognized potential of a grid rather than restricting it to your immediate intention. If this occurs, leave the crystal where it wishes to settle.
10. Join up all the points to activate the grid with the power of your mind or a crystal wand.
11. Add a perimeter or anchor stones if appropriate (see page 35).

TIP:
Handle small crystals with tweezers to make the placement more exact.

1. Gather the tools you will need for laying out and cleansing your grid. Tweezers and a flat blade such as a screwdriver assist in aligning the crystals.

2. Cleanse your crystal thoroughly before use.

3. State your intention for the grid while holding the crystal.

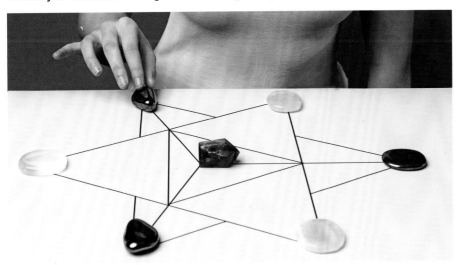

4. Place the major crystals within the grid.

5. Place the keystone in the center of the grid first when radiating energy out.

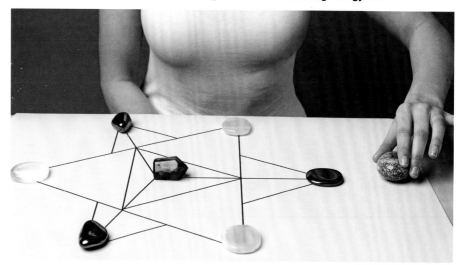

6. Place an anchor stone to ground the grid into everyday reality.

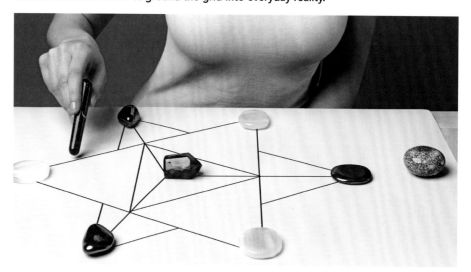

7. Join up the grid with a crystal wand or the power of your mind.

ACTIVATING THE GRID

To activate a grid once it has been laid, use a crystal wand or the power of your mind to join up all the points, including the keystone. If the grid does not have connecting lines to each crystal, take the wand (or your mind) into the central point and out again, touching each crystal in turn and weaving the energy into being. Finally, place the wand on the keystone and restate your intention.

KEEPING THE GRID ACTIVE

Check in with your grid on a regular basis (but don't overdo it!). How often you should check in with your grid depends on its purpose. Some, such as protective or transmuting grids, need daily checking, while outdoor grids or those set to attract abundance can happily be left alone for a week. To keep your grid active, restate your intention, cleanse the crystals if necessary, and remove or add further crystals if appropriate. But don't interfere with your grid too frequently, or you won't really give it a chance to work.

DISMANTLING THE GRID

Once a grid has served its purpose, it can be dismantled. Leaving activated crystals or the imprint of a grid lying around—especially if you go on to create other grids—can create an energetic cacophony where too many energies are "speaking" all at once. To deactivate a grid, cleanse the crystals thoroughly after dismantling (dark and smoky transmuting crystals may benefit from being buried in the earth for a short time if they have been working particularly hard, or from being placed in uncooked brown rice overnight). Then hold the crystals in your hands, saying:

I thank these crystals for their work, which is no longer needed at this time. I ask that the power be closed until reactivated.

Put the crystals in sunlight and/or moonlight to recharge for a few hours or overnight, then place them in a box or a drawer. This effectively puts the crystals to "sleep" until they are required again.

Spray the space in which the grid was laid out with clearing and recharging essence (see page 29). Some layouts create an extremely powerful multi-level energetic imprint that remains long after the grid has been dismantled. While grid imprints with a generalized purpose, such as bringing peace and tranquility or to render support, can be left to dissipate on their own, if a grid has been constructed to alleviate a specific situation or transmute a condition that has now passed, it may need specific energetic deconstruction once it has served its purpose. This deconstruction is especially necessary if you are using high-vibration crystals.

Sound is excellent for closing down such energetic imprints. You may need to sound a drum, Tibetan bowl, tuning forks, or tingshaws over the space to completely close down the grid at all levels. Alternatively, you can smudge the space with sage or sweetgrass.

CREATE YOUR OWN CUSTOM GRID

Once you understand the basic processes and energetic harmonics of grids, you can move on to creating your own. These grids don't need to be complex. A simple heart-shaped grid, for instance, is a potent way to draw love into your life—or to send it into the world. Custom grids can also be created to send healing to a person or to a place. Simply hold that person in your mind as you lay appropriate crystals in place. They will radiate forgiveness, empathy, understanding—whatever the recipient requires. Or, you may see a shape that appeals to you and inspires you to create a grid. It could be a card or tile, a slice of tree, or a geometric form. Simply picture the grid with your mind, or dowse (see page 31) for the position of the crystals, following the procedures for laying a grid that you have already learned.

The base for this heart-shaped grid was found in a junk shop. Although slightly battered, it made the perfect foundation for a grid to heal the heart and attract love.

CHAPTER THREE

THE CHAKRAS AND THE AURA

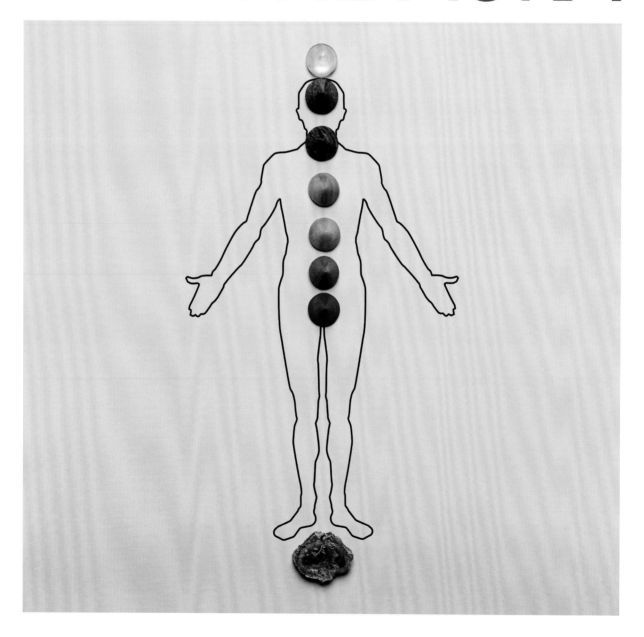

THE CHAKRAS are energy vortexes that link the physical body with the subtle energy bodies (see page 49) and influence specific spheres of life and physiology. They connect to various organs and systems of the body and, if out of balance or blocked, can lead to energetic dis-ease. If this isn't corrected, physical disease may result.

Chakras have been assigned "traditional" color associations, but these are a comparatively recent addition to crystal lore and it is more important to find crystals that are appropriate for your individual needs rather than to follow the color code exactly. Chakra grids can be created by placing crystals on the chakras and anchor stones (on the feet). Grids such as the Tree of Life (see page 127) or the lemniscate (the infinity symbol), are excellent for balancing the chakras.

GAIA GATEWAY

Position: Several feet below the feet

Influence: Planetary connection and anchoring light. Blockages lead to extreme sensitivity to earth changes and to susceptibility to geopathic and electromagnetic stress. Being in incarnation, and especially a physical body, is challenging when this chakra is out of balance. You may not feel at ease in your physical body, or you may experience another kind of discomfort, like a sense of not belonging on the planet. There is no ability to remain stable during periods of energetic shift.

Physiology: The spiritual subtle body and the soul

Typical dis-eases: Inability to assimilate energetic changes and to ground kundalini energy and higher consciousness can lead to varied symptoms of dis-ease. (See *Crystal Prescriptions (Volume 4)* in the Resources section, page 184.)

EARTH STAR

Position: Below the feet

Influence: Everyday reality and groundedness. Imbalances or blockages lead to physical discomfort, feelings of powerlessness, and an inability to function practically or to perform the practical tasks of living, such as showering, paying rent, and caring for children. Imbalances pick up adverse environmental factors, such as geopathic stress and toxic pollutants.

Physiology: Physical body, electrical and meridian systems, sciatic nerve, and sensory organs

Typical dis-eases: Muscular disorders, psychiatric disturbances, auto-immune diseases

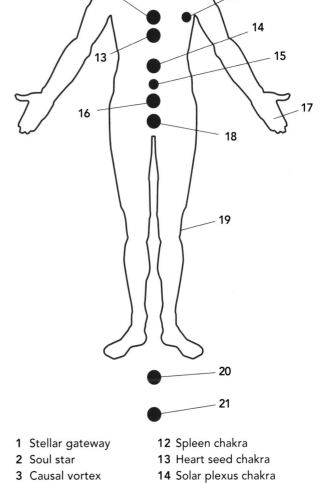

1 Stellar gateway
2 Soul star
3 Causal vortex
4 Crown chakra
5 Soma chakra
6 Third eye chakra
7 Alta major chakra
8 Past life chakra
9 Throat chakra
10 Higher heart chakra
11 Heart chakra
12 Spleen chakra
13 Heart seed chakra
14 Solar plexus chakra
15 Dantien chakra
16 Sacral chakra
17 Palm chakra
18 Base chakra
19 Knee chakra
20 Earth star
21 Gaia gateway

The Chakras and Associated Colors

CHAKRA	COLOR
Gaia gateway	black, gray, metallic, crystalline green
Earth star	brown, dark gray, maroon
Knee	multi-colored, tan, purple
Base	red
Sacral	orange
Dantien	reddish-orange, amber
Solar plexus	yellow, light greenish-yellow
Spleen	green
Heart seed	pale pearlescent blue, pink, white
Heart	green, pink
Higher heart	pink, gold, purple, blue
Palm	silver-white, golden-white, red, blue
Throat	blue, turquoise
Third eye	indigo
Soma	blue, lavender, white, ultra-violet
Crown	white, purple, lavender
Stellar gateway	deep violet, white, gold, silver or clear
Soul star	magenta, white, black
Alta major	magenta, green
Causal vortex	white, gold, light blue

NOTE:
The heart seed, heart, and higher heart chakras together form the three-chambered heart chakra, the sphere of deep compassion and divine love. The three-chambered heart chakra is an integrated chakra that resonates at a very high vibrational frequency to unite all the auric bodies with "above" (celestial energies) and "below" (the earth-plane).

KNEE

Position: Horizontally through the knee caps

Influence: Balance and the ability to nurture and support yourself. Setting realistic goals and manifesting what is needed on a day-to-day basis. Chronic fear and feelings of inferiority, and consequent subservience result from blocked knee chakras. The soul is not grounded into the earth-plane and so feels empty. A blown knee chakra constantly meets problems with authority, authority figures, and bureaucracy.

Physiology: Brain, kidneys, lumbar spine, heart, bladder and kidney meridians, sciatic nerve

Typical dis-eases: Frequent knee problems, arthritis, water on the knee, cartilage and joint problems, bladder problems, cold feet, Osgood-Schlatter disease, bursitis, osteoarthritis, poor leg circulation, sacroiliac pain, lumbar spine, cystitis, eating disorders, malabsorption of nutrients, kidney diseases

BASE

Position: Perineum

Influence: Basic survival instincts and security issues. Imbalances lead to sexual disturbances and feelings of being stuck, anger, impotence, frustration, and an inability to let go. The fight-or-flight response is constantly switched on.

Physiology: Adrenals, bladder, elimination systems, gonads, immune system, kidneys, lower back, lower extremities, sciatic nerve, lymph system, prostate gland, rectum, skeletal system, veins

Endocrine system: Adrenal gland

Typical dis-eases: Stiffness in joints; chronic lower back pain; renal, reproductive, or rectal disorders; glandular disturbances; personality and anxiety disorders; auto-immune diseases

SACRAL

Position: Halfway between base and navel

Influence: Creativity, fertility, and acceptance of oneself as a powerful sexual being. Imbalances lead to infertility and blocked creativity. Emotional "hooks" from other people make themselves felt, particularly from previous sexual encounters.

Physiology: Bladder and gallbladder, immune and elimination systems, kidneys, large and small intestine, lumbar and pelvic region, sacrum, spleen, ovaries, testes, uterus, appetite

Endocrine system: Ovaries and testes

Typical dis-eases: Toxic and psychosomatic, infections, reproductive blockages, addictions, eating disorders, diabetes

DANTIEN

Position: Hand's breadth below the navel

Influence: Power and energy assimilation. Core energy source, inner strength, stability, and balance. Matrilineal and intrauterine issues. If the dantien is too open, you are labile, frenetic, and constantly drained. When it's blocked, lightheadedness, powerlessness, and feeling ill at ease in incarnation result.

Typical dis-eases: Relate to physical function and energy utilization, nervous system dysfunctions, auto-immune diseases, cardiac problems, high blood pressure, adrenal overload, chronic fatigue, myalgic encephalomyelitis, Raynaud's, Parkinson's, digestive problems, diabetes

SOLAR PLEXUS

Position: Hand's breadth above the navel

Influence: Emotional communication and assimilation. Blockages lead to lack of empathy or, if the chakra is too open, taking on other people's feelings and problems, and becoming overwhelmed by personal emotions. Energy assimilation and utilization, and concentration, are poor. Susceptible to emotional "hooks" from other people. "Illness as theater"—that is, illness as a site of, or vehicle for, a repressed personal narrative or ongoing family drama—plays out the story.

Physiology: Adrenals, digestive system, liver, lymphatic system, metabolism, muscles, pancreas, skin, small intestine, stomach, eyesight

Endocrine system: Pancreas

Typical dis-eases: Emotional and demanding, myalgic encephalomyelitis, "fight-or-flight" adrenaline imbalances, insomnia and chronic anxiety, skin conditions, eating disorders and phobias

HEART SEED

Position: Base of breastbone

Influence: Soul remembrance. If blocked, spiritual purpose is lost; one feels rootless and disconnected. Functioning positively, there is awareness of the reason for incarnation and a sense of connection to the divine plan.

Typical dis-eases: Psycho-spiritual, not physical

HEART

Position: Center of chest

Influence: Love and nurturing. If blocked, love cannot flourish. Feelings such as jealousy are common, with enormous resistance to change.

Physiology: Chest, circulation, heart, lungs, shoulders, thymus, respiratory system

Typical dis-eases: Psychosomatic and reactive, heart attacks, angina, chest infections, asthma, frozen shoulder, ulcers

HIGHER HEART (THYMUS)

Position: Midway between base of breastbone and throat

Influence: Compassion and immunity. If blocked, an individual may be emotionally needy and unable to express feelings openly; unconditional love and service cannot be given.

Physiology: Psychic and physical immune systems, thymus gland, lymphatic system, elimination and purification organs

Endocrine system: Thymus

Typical dis-eases: Immune deficiencies, arteriosclerosis, viral infections, tinnitus, epilepsy

SPLEEN

Position: Below left armpit

Influence: Assertion and empowerment. Psychic vampires link in here to get their energy fix. If imbalanced, anger issues or constant irritation may result, or the body turns inward to attack itself. If too open, other people draw energy, causing depletion at the immune level.

Endocrine system: Pancreas

Typical dis-eases: Depletion, lethargy, anemia, low blood sugar

THROAT

Position: Over physical throat

Influence: Communication and self-expression. If blocked, thoughts and feelings cannot be verbalized, nor truth expressed. Other people's opinions cause difficulties.

Physiology: Ears, nose, respiratory and nervous system, sinuses, skin, throat, thyroid, parathyroid, tongue, tonsils, speech and body language, metabolism

Endocrine system: Thyroid/parathyroid

Typical dis-eases: Sore throat/quinsy, inflammation of trachea, sinus, constant colds and viral infections, tinnitus and ear infections, jaw pain and gum disease, tooth problems, thyroid imbalances, high blood pressure, attention-deficit/hyperactivity disorder (ADHD), autism, speech impediments, psychosomatic dis-eases such as irritable bowel

THIRD EYE (BROW)

Position: Above and between eyebrows
Influence: Intuition and mental connection. Imbalances allow bombardment by other people's thoughts or wild and irrational intuitions. Controlling or coercive mental "hooks" from other people lock in and affect thoughts.
Physiology: Brain, ears, eyes, neurological and endocrine systems, pineal and pituitary glands, hypothalamus, production of serotonin and melatonin, temperature control, scalp, sinuses
Endocrine system: Hypothalamus, pituitary gland, medulla oblongata
Typical dis-eases: Migraines, mental overwhelm, schizophrenia, cataracts, iritis and eye problems, epilepsy, autism, spinal and neurological disorders, sinus and ear infections, high blood pressure, "irritations" of all kinds

SOMA

Position: Mid-hairline above third eye
Influence: Soul–body connection, the anchor that holds the subtle energy bodies in contact with the physical self during out-of-body experiences. When activated, the soma chakra opens metaphysical awareness. When this chakra is wide open, it is difficult for the subtle bodies to remain anchored in the physical realm. Spontaneous out-of-body experiences, wild delusions, and frenetic or manic energy results.
Typical dis-eases: Autistic and disconnected or dyspraxic; may include Down syndrome, autism, and ADHD; chronic fatigue, delusional states, sinus or eye problems, migraine headaches, stress headaches, digestive difficulties

PAST LIFE

Position: Behind the ears and along the bony ridge leading to top of spine
Influence: Memory and hereditary issues. Imbalances are stuck in the past and cannot move forward, repeating personal past life patterns or ancestral patterns. People from the past attach and control.
Physiology: Karmic blueprint and etheric bodies
Typical dis-eases: Chronic illnesses, immune or endocrine deficiencies, genetic or physical malfunctions

CROWN

Position: Top of head
Influence: Spiritual communication and awareness. If blocked, attempts to control others are common; if stuck open, obsession and openness to spiritual interference or possession. When imbalanced, excessive environmental sensitivity and delusions or dementia result.
Physiology: Brain, central nervous system, hair, hypothalamus, pituitary gland, spine, subtle energy bodies, cerebellum, nervous motor control, posture and balance
Endocrine system: Pineal
Typical dis-eases: Metabolic syndrome; "dis-ease" with no known cause; nervous system disturbances; electro-magnetic and environmental sensitivity; depression, dementia, myalgic encephalomyelitis, insomnia or excessive sleepiness, "biological clock" disturbances

SOUL STAR

Position: Foot or so above crown
Influence: Soul connection and spiritual illumination. If blocked or stuck open, soul fragmentation occurs. (Soul fragmentation occurs when part of the soul remains "stuck" within, or because of, an unresolved trauma and manifests as the sense of something "missing" in a spiritual sense. A part of the soul may also remain stuck in another life, or in a past trauma—no matter how long ago the trauma occurred.) Spiritually arrogant and may have messianic complex or be open to invasion from "alien" entities.
Physiology: Subtle energy bodies
Typical dis-eases: Spiritual, not physical

STELLAR GATEWAY

Position: One foot or so above soul star

Influence: Cosmic portal. Access to cosmic consciousness. If blocked or stuck open, the individual may become delusional and may contact low-level negative entities—mischievous or malicious spirits who have stayed too close to the earth-plane or other astral beings, including thought forms and the like—disseminating spiritual disinformation.

Physiology: Subtle energy bodies

Typical dis-eases: Spiritual, not physical

CAUSAL VORTEX (GALACTIC)

Position: Above and to the side of the head (dowse to locate the exact site, see page 31)

Influence: Cosmic web and the universal mind. Repository for ancestral and karmic memories. Contains the Akashic record of the soul, a subtle memory bank—rather like the World Wide Web—containing everything that ever has occurred or ever could occur in any timeframe or dimension. When blocked, metaphysical abilities are cut off from the conscious mind but nevertheless affect behavior.

Physiology: Etheric and karmic blueprint, inherited and karmic diseases, DNA and RNA

Typical dis-eases: Inherited, karmic, and cultural

ALTA MAJOR (ASCENSION)

Position: Merkaba shape inside the head (see diagram on page 43)

Influence: Accelerating and expanding consciousness, the soul's plan. This chakra holds the ancestral past and ingrained patterns that govern human life and awareness. In conjunction with the causal vortex and past life chakras, it contains past life karma and contractual agreements made with the higher self and others before present incarnation.

Physiology: Voluntary muscle movements; subtle and physical endocrine systems, including hippocampus, hypothalamus, pineal and pituitary glands; brain function; cerebellum, medulla oblongata (controlling breathing, heart rate, and blood pressure); hormonal balance; occipital area and optic nerve; throat; spine; sleeping patterns

Typical dis-eases: Based on qualities the soul intends to develop, or on balancing the past. For example, if a soul has been "hard-hearted" in the past, then arteriosclerosis—hardening of the arteries—could occur. But if such a soul intended to develop compassion, a quality that was previously missing, then the dis-ease might well be a physically debilitating one such as spina bifida or severe arthritis occurring early in life, so that the soul learns how it feels to experience being "disabled."

PALM

Position: In the palms of the hands and extending up the fingers and arms

Influence: A major factor in interaction with the outside world, the palm chakras mediate the reception and emission of energy.

Physiology: Nerves, tendons, ganglions, skin, hands, fingers, nails

Typical dis-eases: Psychiatric and social dis-ease; skin complaints

THE SUBTLE BODIES AND THE AURA

The physical body is surrounded and interpenetrated by subtle energy fields: the aura or biomagnetic sheath. These bodies are linked through, but not limited to, the chakras. The subtle bodies are blueprints holding information, bio-memory imprints, and energetic remnants from which the physical body is constructed and maintained. Blockages in the chakras can be released by healing the subtle energy body. Conversely, balancing a chakra can clear the subtle energy body. Although shown as bands or "ripples" around the physical body, the seven subtle bodies actually interweave and project several feet out from the physical. This list of subtle bodies is based on how close, or how far, the vibration of those bodies is to that of the physical body. The farther from the body, the higher and finer the vibration.

Physical-etheric body: The "physical" subtle body, or etheric blueprint, is a biomagnetic program that holds imprints of past life dis-ease, injuries, and beliefs that are reflected by present-life symptoms. It also holds subtle DNA that can be activated or switched off by behavior and beliefs, which, in turn, affects DNA in the physical body. This subtle body is connected through the seven traditional, lower-frequency chakras and to the soma, past life, alta major, and causal vortex.

Emotional body: The emotional body is created by emotions and feelings, attitudes, heartbreaks, traumas, and dramas, not only in the present life but also in previous lives. The emotional body contains engrams, which are bundles of energy that hold a deeply traumatic or joyful memory picture. Dis-ease in this body may be reflected in the solar plexus sacral and base chakras, knees, and feet, which act out insecurities and fears. It has a strong connection to the spleen chakra, but also connects to the dantien and navel on the maternal side.

Mental body: The mental body is created by thoughts, memories, credos, and ingrained beliefs from the present and previous lives. It is connected particularly through the throat and head chakras but may be reflected in the lower-body chakras. For example, thoughts and beliefs have a profound effect on sexual functioning, because the lower chakras are where these beliefs are acted out in the world. This is the basis of all psychosomatic "dis-ease," and when "higher principles" conflict with basic bodily needs, endless confusion can result. This body holds the imprint of all that has been said or taught by authority figures in the past, along with inculcated ideologies and points of view.

Karmic body: The karmic body or blueprint holds the imprint of all previous lives and the purpose for the present life. It contains mental programs, physical imprints, and emotional impressions and beliefs—many of which may be contradictory, since they arise from very different experiences in various lives. This body is accessed through the past life, alta major, and causal vortex chakras, but may affect the soma, knee, and Earth star.

Ancestral body: This body holds everything inherited down the ancestral lines on both sides, at both the physical and more subtle levels. This may include family sagas, belief systems and attitudes, culture and expectations, and traumas and dramas. This body can be accessed through the soul star, causal vortex, past life, alta major, higher heart, Earth star, and Gaia gateway chakras.

Planetary body: A subtle energy body that links into the planet and the Earth's etheric body and meridians. This planetary body is connected to the wider cosmos, the luminaries, planets, and stellar bodies, and the outer reaches of the universe: the wider whole. The planetary body is reflected in a birth chart and is accessed through the past life, alta major, causal vortex, soma, stellar, and Gaia gateway chakras. Cosmic or soul dis-ease can be corrected through the planetary subtle body.

Spiritual or Lightbody: An integrated, luminous, vibrating energy field consisting of the physical body and all the subtle energy bodies, plus the spirit or soul, connected through the soma, soul star, stellar gateway, Gaia gateway, alta major, and causal vortex. The spiritual body resonates with the universe, the universal mind, and with the personal soul or spirit.

CHAPTER FOUR

BASIC GRIDS

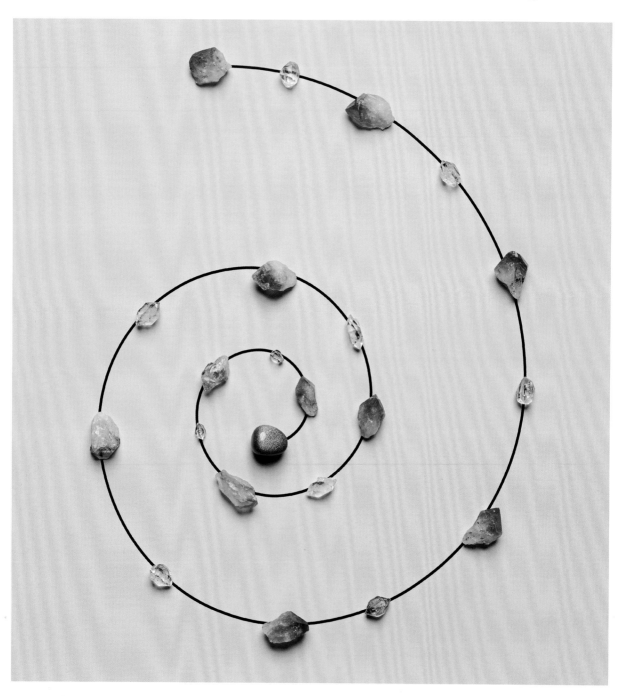

THE GRIDS IN THIS SECTION are deceptively simple, often requiring only a handful of crystals. Nevertheless, they are extremely powerful since a grid's energetic net spreads itself far and wide unless contained by a perimeter. And as you'll see, some basic grids can be extended into other more complex and equally potent forms.

In most cases, there will be no set number of crystals in a grid, nor one set way to lay it. The number of crystals to be used in a grid will vary according to their size and properties, and with the way in which they align with your intention—and with each other. Use your intuition, or dowse (see page 31), to find the type and number of crystals to assist you in a particular grid—and to determine exactly which grid is right for your purpose. I used to believe it was important to have all the crystals exactly aligned in a grid. Experience has taught me that sometimes the crystals will deliberately move out of alignment to create a space for something new to emerge. The grids may need to have slight imperfections in the energetic net to allow change to take place and possibilities to open up. If the grids are always precise and static, the outcome will always be the same. But opening a "slightly flawed space" activates the potential for what I always ask of a grid—"that or something better"—which I add to my intention statement. Crystals are wise, intelligent beings and they can see a lot further than we humans can. I've learned that if a crystal constantly shifts its position in the grid, it's saying loud and clear, "This is where I need to be." Or, if it falls on the floor, it may be saying, "Choose another crystal." Another lesson in listening to the crystals rather than following the rules. The more you work with crystals and grids, the more your skills will develop, so you'll soon be able to sense crystals' energetic effects and to intuitively know what a grid requires. Finally, remember to always use cleansed and dedicated crystals for your grids.

VESICA PISCIS

Vesica Piscis

Continuous Vesica Piscis

NOTE:
Also see page
170 to discover
how to use the
Vesica Piscis to
create harmonious
relationships.

CREATION AND MANIFESTATION

Known as "the womb of the universe," the Vesica Piscis symbolizes the Hermetic axiom "as above, so below; as within, so without." A mystical conjunction, it is consciousness knowing itself and taking on form. This grid represents both unity and "common ground," but the shape also represents separation into component parts. It is the start of life, thus the sphere of creation and manifestation. When you're laying the crystals, alternate different types, or lay a circle of each with a keystone in the center.

Form: The Vesica Piscis is formed from two intersecting circles precisely aligned so that the circumference of one circle exactly touches the center point of the other. The circle is the simplest and yet most profound of forms, for it has no beginning and no end, and encompasses all possibilities. It is the ultimate expression of unity. Overlap the circles, however, and the Vesica Piscis gives birth to the triangle, the square, the hexagon, the Seed of Life, and the Flower of Life.

Uses: Lay the grid upright to draw energy down, or lay it sideways to integrate or to create energy. A symbol of unification and harmony, the Vesica Piscis bridges the spiritual and the physical. It blends logic, intuition, and emotion, or past, present, and future. This grid is excellent for conception, collaboration, conflict resolution, and finding common ground. It is extremely helpful when starting new ventures. Place a keystone in the center to symbolize your purpose.

Timing: Spring is ideal. Place the Vesica Piscis at a new moon when you're starting a fresh venture. A full moon is the most providential for conflict resolution and the integration of opposing forces, but this grid can be placed immediately if you encounter a crisis.

YOU WILL NEED:

- Sufficient crystals to create both circles
- A keystone for the center

TO LAY THE GRID:

1. Hold your crystals in your hands and state your intention for the grid.
2. Lay the left-hand or bottom circle first, carefully aligning the crystals around the circle.
3. Lay the right-hand or top circle.
4. Place your keystone in the center, stating your intention once more.
5. Join the circles with a wand or the power of your mind.
6. When you're ready to dismantle the grid, follow the instructions on page 39.

CONTINUOUS VESICA PISCIS

Place your crystals from the top point down and place a keystone in the central portion of the grid. Anchor stones at the bottom corners ground the energy into place.

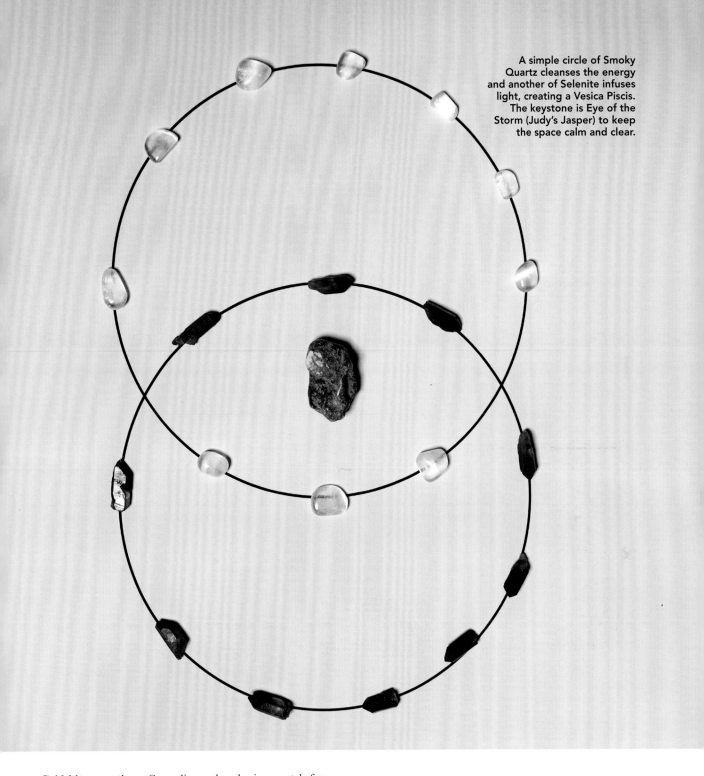

A simple circle of Smoky Quartz cleanses the energy and another of Selenite infuses light, creating a Vesica Piscis. The keystone is Eye of the Storm (Judy's Jasper) to keep the space calm and clear.

Grid-kit suggestions: Grounding and anchoring crystals for the left-hand or bottom circle (see page 30); high-vibration light-bringing crystals for the right-hand or top circle (see page 30). Eye of the Storm (Judy's Jasper), Rose Quartz, Smoky Quartz, or Menalite for fertility

LEMNISCATE (FIGURE OF EIGHT)

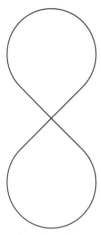

Lemniscate

GROUNDING AND UNIFYING

The lemniscate is a symbol of infinity. Two become one in a sign that stands for wholeness and completion. The loops also reflect the balance of opposites: male and female, day and night, dark and light. This symbol also depicts perpetual motion and the interaction of energy and matter—that is, their indestructibility and their potential for transmutation. It is the "ouroboros," a mythological serpent that devours its own tail in order to sustain life in an eternal cycle of renewal. After all, an ending is also a beginning, and a beginning needs an ending in order to begin again. The term "infinity" was derived from the Latin word *infinitas*, which translates as "unboundedness." Indeed, this grid can be energetically expanded without limit.

Form: The lemniscate is composed of two circles in the same plane, drawn with a continuous line to create a figure of eight. It is a "seesaw" of clockwise and counterclockwise loops with a balance point in the center. The lemniscate can be used pointing upward to draw energy to a central point, or placed sideways to create a continuous flow.

Uses: The lemniscate is an excellent rebalancing layout, particularly suited for placement on and around the human body. The grid both cleanses and draws in light to fill the vacuum created by the release of toxic energies. It can be used for situations in which two separate parts need to be drawn together, since infinity includes all time—past, present, and future—centered in the "now." The lemniscate grid actualizes intention into the present moment. Lay clearing crystals on the lower half and light-bringers on the top loop, and use over the heart seed, heart, and higher heart chakras (the three-chambered heart, see page 44) as an immune stimulator or soother.

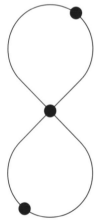

Simplified lemniscate

Timing: No special timing is required. Use the lemniscate whenever it is needed.

YOU WILL NEED:
- Sufficient cleansing and light-bringing crystals for each loop
- An appropriate keystone for the crossing point
- If using around or on the body, a grounding anchor stone

TO LAY THE GRID:
1. Hold your crystals in your hands and state your intention for the grid.
2. If you're laying the grid around your own body, ask an assistant to place the crystals for you.
3. Either place the keystone on your navel or in the center of the grid.
4. Lay the lower loop with cleansing and grounding crystals.
5. Lay the upper loop with energizing and light-bringing crystals.
6. Join up the grid with the power of your mind or a crystal wand.
7. When you're ready to dismantle the grid, follow the instructions on page 39.

Selenite above Smoky Quartz linked by an Eye of the Storm (Judy's Jasper) keystone that also acts as a stabilizing anchor.

Grid-kit suggestions: Grounding and anchoring crystals for the left-hand or upper circle (see page 30); high-vibration light-bringing crystals for the right-hand or lower circle (see page 30). Mookaite Jasper, Porcelain Jasper
Heart grid: Emerald or Fuchsite for the upper circle; Lepidolite or Ruby for the base

THE SIMPLIFIED LEMNISCATE LAYOUT

This layout is useful if you wish to lay the grid on yourself but have no one to assist you. Place a high-vibration crystal such as Anandalite™ over your head and slightly to one side (the opposite side to your dominant hand); a grounding crystal such as Flint beneath your feet and slightly to the opposite side; and an anchor stone that represents your intention over your navel. Check to see if this feels balanced and centered. (You may prefer to place the crystals immediately above your head and below your feet and over the solar plexus.) Join up the crystals with the power of your mind.

TRIANGLE

TRANQUILITY, PROTECTION, AND MANIFESTATION

A triangle is one of the basic forms of life, a foundation of creation. Pythagoras stated that all things emanate from a single point and used the Tetractys triangle (see below) as an example. A triangle represents that which is solid, substantial, and complete in itself. As a grid, however, it not only protects that which is inside it—making it a useful protection mechanism—but also radiates energy out to fill a space and transmute energies. Triangular grids are excellent for smoothing discord and instilling the strength to overcome. A triangular grid can replicate itself endlessly (see below).

Form: Triangles have three sides and three angles, but take several forms. An equilateral triangle has equal sides and angles; an isosceles triangle has two equal sides and two equal angles; and a scalene triangle has three unequal sides and three unequal angles. The "Golden Triangle" is generated from the Golden Ratio spiral (see page 18). The angles and sides arising from the shortest side are equal.

Uses: Excellent for protecting a space, triangular grids can be laid wherever there is disharmony, where protection is required, or where energy requires transmutation. It effortlessly expands to fill the space, so it is particularly effective for small long-term grids. Like the lemniscate, a triangular grid blends logic, intuition, and emotion; mind, body, and spirit; past, present, and future; thought, word, and deed.

Timing: Lay your triangular grid as required. Replenish and cleanse at new and full moon.

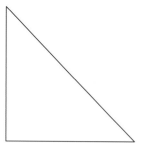

Equilateral triangle

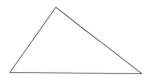

Isosceles triangle

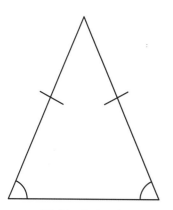

Scalene triangle

"Golden" triangle

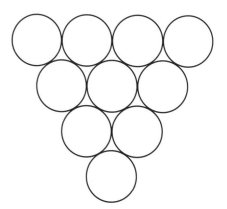

Energetic effect.
In a triangular grid, the energy builds and expands both inward and outward to fill the whole space and create a protective energy field around the area.

Tetractys triangle

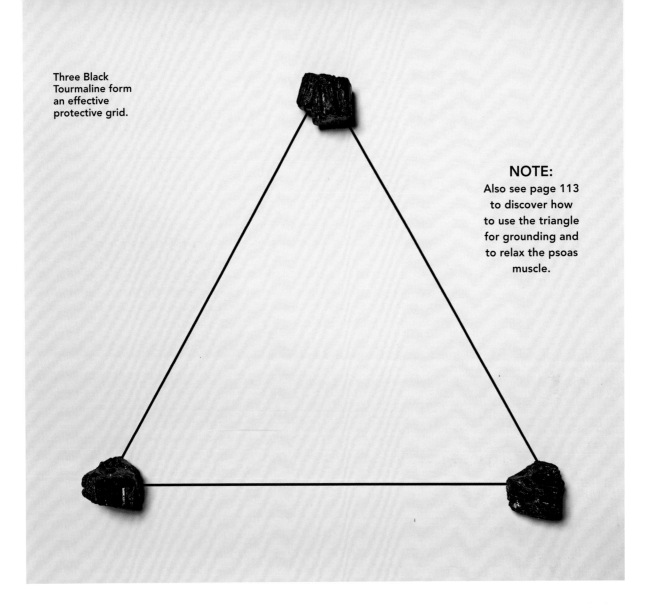

Three Black Tourmaline form an effective protective grid.

NOTE:
Also see page 113 to discover how to use the triangle for grounding and to relax the psoas muscle.

YOU WILL NEED:
- 3 fairly large, appropriate grid crystals

TO LAY THE GRID:
1. Hold your crystals in your hands and state your intention for the grid.
2. If protecting your space, place one crystal centrally along a wall or boundary, or the smaller area on which you are laying your grid, such as a bedside table, for example.
3. Place a crystal in each of the opposite corners of the room or space.
4. Link up the crystals with a crystal wand or the power of your mind.
5. When you're ready to dismantle the grid, follow the instructions on page 39.

Grid-kit suggestions: Grounding, protective, and anchoring crystals (see page 30); high-vibration light-bringing crystals (see page 30); Shungite, Black Tourmaline, Carnelian, Mookaite Jasper, Polychrome Jasper, or Selenite

EXTENDED LAYOUTS

The pentagram and hexagram grids on pages 58 and 60 are extended triangles. And a "solid" Tetractys triangle actualizes your intention. Start with the outer crystals, and then fill in the circles as shown (opposite).

PENTAGRAM (FIVE-POINTED STAR)

ABUNDANCE AND ATTRACTION

Upright pentagram

Inverted pentagram

A pentagram draws the assistance of the gods—archetypal, universal forces—from "above" to down "below," infusing Earthly projects with creative and protective power. It has no innate connection to the dark side, contrary to what superstitious people may say. Intention and purpose are what give a grid its "good" or "not-good" power, not the shape of the grid itself. The upward point represents spirit, while the other four points represent the elements of earth, air, fire, and water, all of which are united in this form. Leonardo da Vinci recognized the pentagram as "Vitruvian man," the human being as a microcosm of the macrocosm—that is, of the universe. It represents the descent of a spark of the divine into tangible matter.

Form: A pentagram is drawn with a continuous, flowing line in five straight strokes—in whichever direction feels most comfortable—creating a five-pointed star. The five spiked "arms" enclose a central "womb," creating a defensive, protective pentagon at the center. The pentagram can be placed into a circle to further strengthen the protection it offers.

Uses: The pentagram has long been believed to be a potent source of protection against evil, acting as a shield that defends the wearer, home, or environment from negative energy. It is also traditionally used to attract abundance and prosperity. An inverted pentagram is helpful for looking deep into oneself, or for transmuting toxic matter, because it draws an element and its properties—such as the cleansing and replenishing power of water—to where it is needed.

Timing: No special timing is required. Lay the pentagram whenever it is needed. If you are using it to attract abundance or when commencing a new project, lay the grid at a new moon or in the spring. Lay it on the summer solstice to bring fresh vitality into your life, or at the winter solstice to transmute toxic patterns and begin a new cycle.

YOU WILL NEED:
- 5 appropriate crystals
- 1 keystone for the center

TO LAY THE GRID:
1. Hold your cleansed crystals in your hands and state your intention for the grid.
2. Place the first crystal at the top point.
3. Follow the line down to place the second crystal at the bottom.
4. Place the third crystal up and across.
5. Place the fourth crystal straight across.
6. Place the fifth crystal down at the remaining bottom point.
7. Join up the crystals with the power of your mind, remembering to return to your starting point.

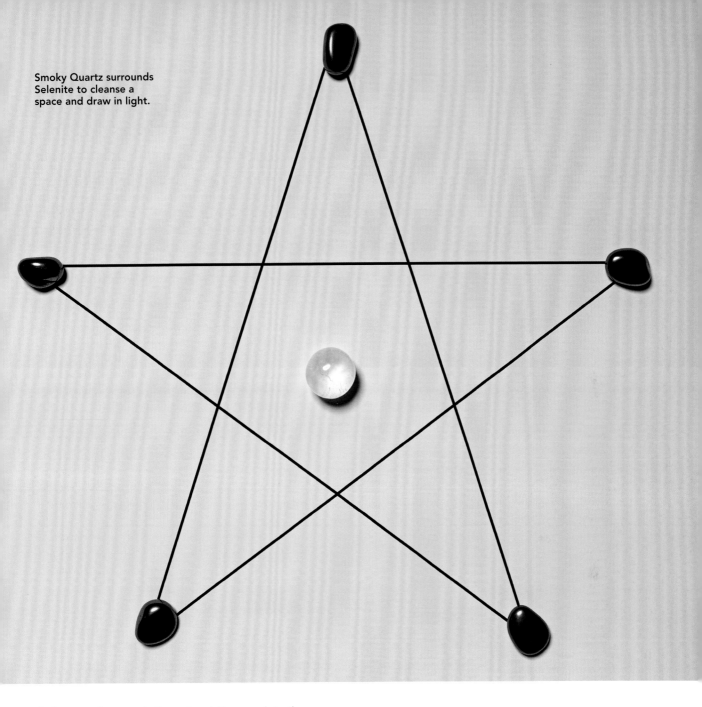

Smoky Quartz surrounds Selenite to cleanse a space and draw in light.

8. Lay your keystone in the center, stating your intention once more.
9. When you're ready to dismantle the grid, follow the instructions on page 39.

Grid-kit suggestions: Grounding, protective, and anchoring crystals; cleansing crystals; high-vibration light-bringing crystals; abundance crystals (see page 30)

HEXAGRAM

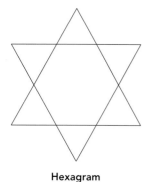

Hexagram

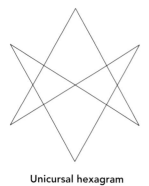

Unicursal hexagram

NOTE:
See page 22 to discover how to use the Unicursal hexagram for clearing EMF smog.

PROTECTION AND CLEANSING

Known as the "Creator's Star," the "Star of David," or "Solomon's Seal," the hexagram is another ancient symbol of protection and of the unification of opposing forces. The symbol for the heart chakra is a hexagram. At the junction of heaven and earth, it balances the primary emotional energy of the universe—love. It reminds us that we are children of both spirit and earth. While it has many occult uses, the symbol itself is neutral (like the pentagram); it is the use to which it is put that adds a specific positive or negative power. The hexagram's six points are said to stand for the six days of creation, and to represent the six attributes of God: power, wisdom, majesty, love, mercy, and justice.

Form: Two interlocked, overlapping equilateral triangles create the perfect hexagram, but they can be extended to fill a space. A unicursal hexagram is drawn with a single line, and it is particularly useful for unification grids.

Uses: This grid balances internal and external needs and desires. The first triangle draws down light and then locks it into place, while the second triangle clears toxicity and grounds energy. It is an excellent symbol of protection. Place the name or photograph of a person who needs assistance into the center under the keystone, and the protective energy will be transmitted to them. Sitting within a hexagram can also clear mind chatter and help overcome insomnia, especially if the grid is created from Auralite 23 or Amethyst.

Timing: No special timing is required. Lay the hexagram whenever it is needed.

YOU WILL NEED:

- 3 clearing crystals
- 3 light-bringing crystals
- 1 Keystone for the center

TO LAY THE GRID:

1. Hold your crystals in your hands and state your intention for the grid.
2. Lay the first triangle, placing clearing crystals on each point.
3. Join up the points and spray the grid with clearing essence. (Dowse, see page 31, to see whether the triangle should point up or down.)
4. Lay the light-bringing crystals in an overlocking triangle over the top of the first. Join up the points, starting with the first crystal you laid.
5. Place your keystone in the center, stating your intention once more. When you're ready to dismantle the grid, follow the instructions on page 39.

Grid-kit suggestions: Grounding, protective, and anchoring or cleansing crystals in the downward triangle. High-vibration, light-bringing crystals or abundance crystals in upward triangle (see page 30).

An Amethyst and
Snow Quartz keystone
surrounded by Selenite
to infuse light and
mutual understanding
into a neighborhood.

SQUARE

BALANCING AND SOLIDIFYING

Square

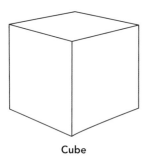

Cube

Rectangle and
parallelograms

The square template is one of the most basic and versatile of grids. A configuration with perfect symmetry, it anchors intention and grounds energy. In its simplest form, it is created by placing a crystal in the four corners of a room or at the four corners of a bed. But a square grid's power isn't limited to its perimeters. It creates an energetic cube, so it can be used to grid a building or another specific site. As a protective layout, the square grid consolidates energy, balancing and solidifying it. It also repels detrimental energies and so creates a contained, safe space. The grid can be extended by placing anchoring crystals outside the square (see page 173), which holds grid energy in place for long periods of time and is particularly useful for gridding a house.

Form: Strictly speaking, a square has four equal sides and four equal angles. However, this template can be adapted to fit the shape of a space. It can be extended on two sides to become a rectangle, or slanted to create a parallelogram. Not all of the square's sides and angles have to remain equal for the energetic effect to become apparent.

Uses: A square layout protects a space from geopathic stress or electromagnetic pollution, and it also creates a safe space in which to live, work, or meditate. Place it around your bed if you have trouble sleeping, or around a room to calm the atmosphere and reduce noise levels—or, place it on and around your head to create clarity. The square is also used in situations where limits need to be defined, or where out-of-control energy needs to be contained. Finally, squares are excellent for aligning goals and building community.

Timing: No special timing is required. Lay a square grid whenever it is needed.

YOU WILL NEED:
- 4 crystals of similar type and size
- Keystone for the center, if appropriate

TO LAY THE GRID:
1. Hold your crystals in your hands and state your intention for the grid.
2. Lay your first crystal in one corner. (Dowse, see page 31, to see which crystal should be the first one laid.)
3. Lay your second crystal in the corner to the right of the first.
4. Lay your third crystal below that in the next corner.
5. Lay your final crystal in the last corner.
6. Join up the corners and the crystals with a wand or the power of your mind. Feel the energy pinging around the grid as you do so, lighting it up.
7. If appropriate, lay a keystone as close to the center as possible to anchor the energy. The activation is now complete.

NOTE:
See page 172 to discover how to use the square to protect against EMFs and page 134 to gain clarity.

Shungite placed in the four corners provides protection against EMF pollution and dissipates toxic earth energies.

8. Leave the grid in place for as long as necessary. This is a long-term protection grid, so you may leave it in place for many months. Cleanse as often as necessary.
9. When you're ready to dismantle the grid, follow the instructions on page 39.

Grid-kit suggestions: Grounding, protective, anchoring, or cleansing crystals (see page 30). Shungite with Herkimer Diamond is especially appropriate for this grid if your intention is to protect against electric and magnetic fields.

ZIGZAG

ENVIRONMENTAL CLEANSING

A zigzag structure is inherently more stable than a straight line; it's better able to absorb stresses, maintaining its high-energy output. It is ideal for laying around or within a building to create protection and to discharge static or electromagnetic smog.

Form: A line of crystals is laid along a boundary wall from one end to the other in a zigzag fashion. To protect or clear the space, another line is laid along the opposite wall. (This double line is more powerful than a single one because it contains the energy within the space being encompassed.) The crystals can be alternated. Place clearing crystals on the top edge of the zig, and light-bringing crystals on the zag.

Uses: The zigzag layout is particularly useful for healing sick-building syndrome (see page 183) and neutralizing environmental pollution. It is also helpful if you want to clear clutter, or energetically declutter a space.

Timing: No special timing is required. Lay the grid whenever it is necessary.

Zigzag

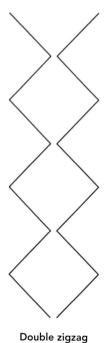

Double zigzag

The energetic effect. When a double zigzag is laid, the energy moves toward the center of the grid to fill the whole area with protective, transmuting energy.

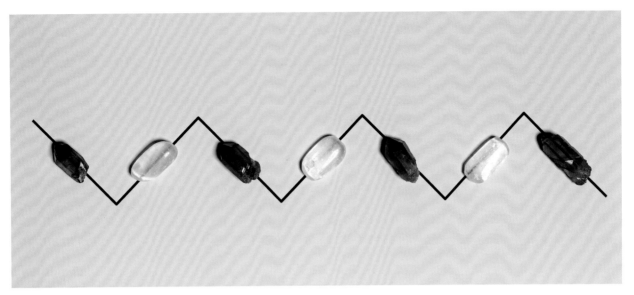

Smoky Quartz and Selenite are an ideal combination for healing sick-building syndrome.

YOU WILL NEED:

- Sufficient crystals to run the length of the wall at regular intervals, depending on the length of the wall
- An anchor stone can be placed at each end

TO LAY THE GRID:

1. Hold your crystals in your hands and state your intention for the grid.
2. Lay the first crystal against the left-hand wall. Begin with an anchor stone, if appropriate (use your intuition to decide).
3. Lay a zigzag all the way to the right-hand wall. Place an anchor stone at the end if this is appropriate.
4. If creating the double zigzag, move to the opposite wall and repeat the operation.
5. Join up the crystals with the power of your mind or a crystal wand. (If making a double zigzag, walk from one end to the other, and then back to the starting point.)
6. When you're ready to dismantle the grid, follow the instructions on page 39.

Grid-kit suggestions: Black Tourmaline, Shungite, Smoky Quartz, Herkimer Diamond, Selenite, Quartz

SPIRAL

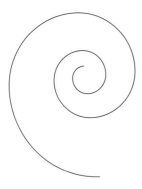

Spiral

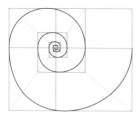

Golden Ratio spiral

VORTEX ENERGY MANAGEMENT

A spiral is one of the foundational forms in which organisms grow. It creates vortex energy—that is, a whirling mass of energy generated from a central point and either radiated outward or sucked inward, depending on its electrostatic charge—and is a basis for accelerating growth and switching on positive DNA potential. Depending on which way it is placed, a spiral draws energy down into its center—a crystal placed at the top begins the process—or radiates energy from a crystal placed at its center. So, when you're joining the crystals with your wand or the power of your mind, do not go back to the first crystal you laid. Instead, depending on your intention, spiral the energy out and away or down into the spiral's center. You can also use a multi-armed spiral (see the complex grid on page 101) when you want to radiate transmuting and re-energizing vibrations out into the surrounding area for as great a distance as possible.

Form: You could lay a "perfect logarithmic spiral" using the Golden Ratio (see the illustration at left), but this is not essential for grid work. Instead, dowse (see page 31) or use your intuition to check whether you should be using a clockwise or counterclockwise spiral and how many crystals are needed for your grid.

Uses: A spiral re-energizes a space or helps to begin a project, sending the idea out into the universe ahead of you. Use it also to irradiate a "dead" or empty space with crystal energy, especially after energetic clearing has taken place. This is a particularly useful grid for map or photographic work.

Timing: Lay a spiral grid at any time. However, a drawing-down or inward grid is particularly potent at new moon, and a radiating one is most powerful at full moon.

YOU WILL NEED:

- Sufficient crystals to outline the spiral.
- Keystone for the center, or the end.

TO LAY THE GRID:

NOTE:
See page 140 to discover how to use the spiral for abundance.

1. Create your spiral. (A piece of string is ideal for creating the form.)
2. Hold your crystals in your hands and state your intention for the grid.
3. Place the first crystal (the keystone) at the center or at the end, depending on your intention. (If you're drawing in energy, you'll lay the outer stone first; if you're radiating it, lay the center stone first.)

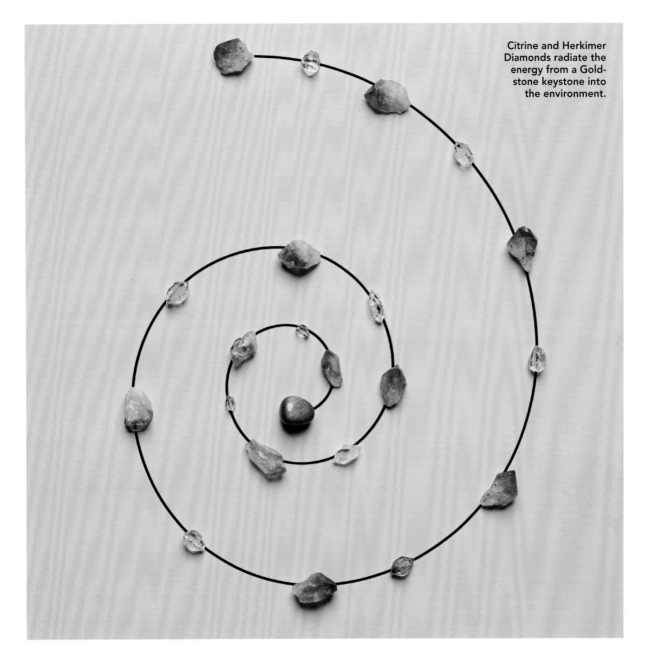

Citrine and Herkimer Diamonds radiate the energy from a Goldstone keystone into the environment.

4. Complete the spiral, laying crystals along it at intervals.
5. Join up the spiral with the power of your mind or a crystal wand, remembering not to return to your starting point. If you began at the center, draw the wand out and away. If you began at the outer edge, tap the wand firmly at the center and then place the keystone there.
6. When you're ready to dismantle the grid, follow the instructions on page 39.

Grid-kit suggestions: Citrine, Herkimer Diamond, Selenite, Sunstone, Goldstone, Smoky Quartz

SUNBURST

ENERGIZING AND REVITALIZING

As its name suggests, a sunburst layout is highly energizing, and it radiates its energy over a large area, so it is particularly suited to placement on the ground or over a map. Although it's typical to start laying crystals in the center of the sunburst and to work outward from there, it can be helpful to dowse (see page 31) or use your intuition for the placements of crystals before you begin. This is because a directional alignment—that is, one that's aligned to the points of the compass—may need to be set out first, and the central stone could be laid first or last according to whether the crystals are placed to draw energy in or out. The layout can always be adjusted later to fine-tune the energies.

Unlike many other grids, this layout is not activated by joining with a wand, as the intention is to radiate the energy as widely as possible. Instead, a radiating sunburst is set in motion by the intention of your mind. When you're placing the crystals, remember that points channel energy in the direction in which they face. If a point is facing toward you or to a specific spot, it channels energy in to you or to that spot. If it's pointing away from you, it sends energy outward.

Form: A sunburst grid can have short or long arms, and they may be equal or unequal, or a mixture of both. Crystals can be laid in lines, or simply placed at each end around a central keystone. It can be as large or as small as you wish. If you're building a large sunburst to remain in place over time, use large raw crystals and ensure that they can be cleansed and energized as appropriate. Or, soak them in Petaltone Z14 if you intend to bury them in the ground. (Always be sure to mark where such a grid lies.)

Uses: First and foremost, sunburst grids are energizing grids. But they can have other functions, too. A sunburst can be built of detoxifying crystals, offering ongoing cleansing and protection to an area that's particularly or regularly polluted, for example. It can also be used to direct energy away from a particular space by placing protective crystals pointing toward the center on the side that needs shielding, and by placing radiating crystals pointing away from the center on the opposite side. And, finally, a radiating sunburst can send healing over huge distances to a specific recipient (see page 174).

Timing: Lay a sunburst grid at any time. However, it is particularly potent in the spring, for energizing, and before winter, for detoxifying.

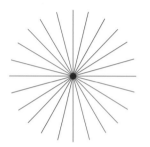

Sunburst with unequal arms

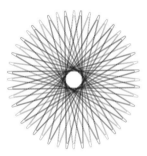

Equal-armed sunburst

Energetic effect.
A sunburst grid doesn't just emit straight lines of energy; it also creates an interlocking energy grid that either radiates or draws in energy, according to the direction in which the crystals face.

Citrine and Smoky
Quartz radiate the
vibrant energy of
a Tangerine Sun
Aura Quartz into
the environment.

YOU WILL NEED:

- Sufficient crystals for your purpose (dowse, see page 31, before beginning to determine exactly how many and which kind)

TO LAY THE GRID:

1. Hold your crystals in your hands, and state your intention for the grid.
2. Dowse (see page 31) or use your intuition for the appropriate positions for your cleansed crystals, and lay them roughly in a sunburst shape. You don't necessarily need to lay the central keystone first. Trust your intuition to tell you when to place it in your grid.
3. Stand at the center of the grid (or focus your attention into its center) and state your intention.
4. Fine-tune the grid by aligning crystals carefully or allowing them to roll into the position they choose.
5. Check that the final placements are effective by dowsing or using your intuition.
6. Activate the grid with the power of your mind.
7. When you're ready to dismantle the grid, follow the instructions on page 39.

NOTE:
See page 174 for a
further example of
the sunburst grid.

Grid-kit suggestions: Carnelian, Celtic Quartz, Citrine, Quartz, Red Jasper, Sunstone, Smoky Quartz, Shungite, Flint, Hematite

CRYSTAL GLOSSARY

CITRINE

Citrine gives you energy to manifest your own reality and to attract everything you need. It invigorates the body and activates the immune system. Beneficial for degenerative dis-eases, it encourages energy flow and balances hormones.

SMOKY QUARTZ

This versatile healing crystal carries the underlying properties of Quartz. It works on the kidneys and other organs of elimination to remove toxins from the body. An excellent grounding stone for rebalancing the body, Smoky Quartz strengthens underlying core stability and prevents healing crises from occurring. In a healing grid, Smoky Quartz absorbs disharmonious environmental energy. With the point facing out, it transmutes negative energy and draws in healing light.

SUNSTONE

A powerfully energizing stone, Sunstone infuses the light of the sun into an area or a physical body, revitalizing it instantly. It is particularly useful in the dark days of winter.

RED JASPER

Connected with the base chakra, courageous Red Jasper is a physically invigorating stone that imparts vitality and optimism. It replenishes lost energy and can energize a whole grid.

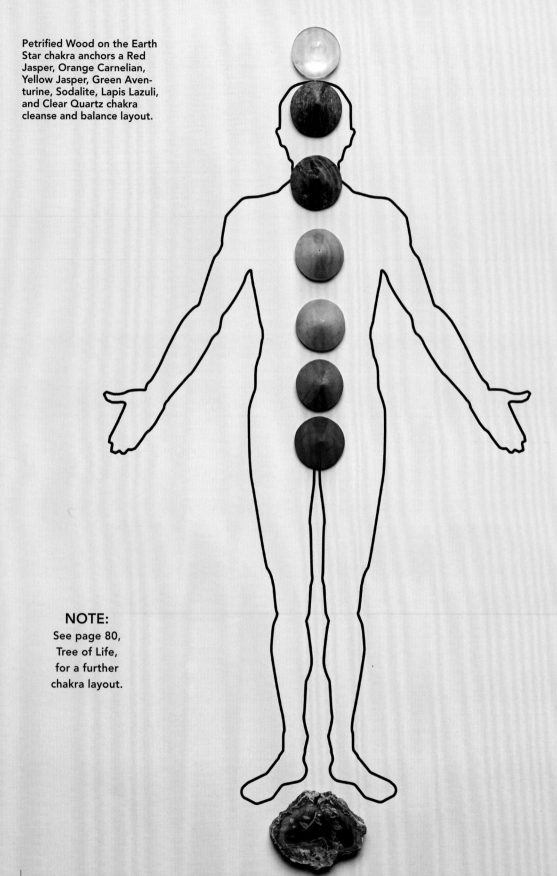

Petrified Wood on the Earth Star chakra anchors a Red Jasper, Orange Carnelian, Yellow Jasper, Green Aventurine, Sodalite, Lapis Lazuli, and Clear Quartz chakra cleanse and balance layout.

NOTE:
See page 80,
Tree of Life,
for a further
chakra layout.

THE BODY

HEALING AND REBALANCING

Your body itself is a grid. Crystals can be placed on the chakras to cleanse and rebalance them, and they can be placed on and around the body—and over specific organs—to restore well-being. For example, when laid around the head, crystals such as Auralite 23 are particularly effective for shutting off mind chatter to create a quiet mind and to reduce stress (see page 132). This can also help to overcome insomnia. Crystals placed over the kidneys and adrenals switch off the fight-or-flight response, and stress can also be relieved via the psoas muscle relaxer (see example grid on page 113).

Form: Appropriate crystals can be laid on the body, moving upward from feet to head to create a chakra grid, or placed on and around the body as required. The Tree of Life grid (see page 80), for instance, is particularly effective when laid over the body. And one of the most potent physical grids is also one of the simplest. It requires only one stone over the higher heart chakra to stimulate the immune system, and one grounding stone, such as Flint or Smoky Quartz, at the feet. Use Bloodstone, Quantum Quattro, or a dowsed stone.

Timing: Lay a grid whenever necessary, or at new moon for a thorough chakra cleanse and recharge.

YOU WILL NEED:

- Appropriate chakra or healing crystals

TO LAY THE GRID:

1. Choose a place and time when you will not be disturbed. Be sure to switch off your mobile phone.
2. Hold your crystals in your hands, and state your intention for the grid.
3. Lie down and cover yourself with a blanket, if necessary, so that you are warm and comfortable.
4. To lay a grid on or around a physical body, dowse (see page 31) or intuit where each crystal should go, and choose crystals by the same method. You could, for instance, place an appropriate crystal on each chakra. You can also lay a crystal directly over an organ or position it over a specific place, such as the throat, or place the crystals around your head to shut off mind chatter and overcome insomnia. If you are laying the grid on yourself, start with your feet and work upward. Ensure that you have placed a grounding and transmuting crystal below your feet.
5. Leave the grid in place for 10 to 20 minutes.
6. Gather up the crystals in the reverse order in which you placed them. Follow the instructions for dismantling the grid on page 39.

Grid-kit suggestions: Flint, Smoky Quartz, Red Jasper, Carnelian, Yellow Calcite, Green Aventurine, Blue Lace Agate, Lapis Lazuli, Quartz, Blue Kyanite, Polychrome Jasper, Mookaite Jasper, Shungite, Quantum Quattro, Bloodstone, Que Sera. (For healing crystals, see page 30. For chakra colors, see page 44.)

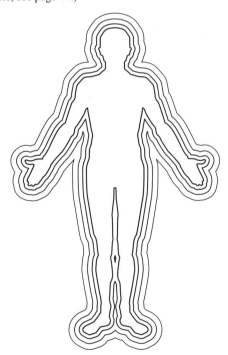

The physical and subtle bodies

CHAPTER FIVE

ADVANCED GRIDS

THE ADVANCED GRIDS IN THIS SECTION may look complicated, but they are just as easy to set out as the basic grids in Chapter 4. Simply follow the templates. With one or two exceptions, such as the Tree of Life (see page 80), they are more suitable for placing in the home, the environment, or around the body rather than on the body itself, but all of them are extremely versatile. Some of the more complex grids create very powerful energetic patterns and are more suitable for use by experienced crystal workers. Such grids may require careful dismantling when their task is complete (see page 39), as the energetic imprint of these grids lasts much longer because of the complex geometry involved in the energetic net. Other grids can be left in the ether (energetic space) to naturally dissipate once the crystals have been removed. It all depends on the purpose for which they have been laid. If a grid has been laid to resolve a specific confrontation, for instance, once that conflict is over, the grid needs to be energetically dismantled. But if the grid is to instill long-lasting peace into an environment or ongoing situation, it can be left to dissipate naturally once the crystals have been removed.

FLOWER OF LIFE

THE FOUNDATION OF CREATION

The Flower of Life is one of the oldest sacred symbols in the world. It has been regarded as a symbol of self-knowledge—and knowledge of the universe as a whole—for thousands of years. For this grid, precise placement of crystals is necessary to control the flow of energy along the pathways—although, occasionally, a crystal will roll out of line to create the space for something new to occur. If you realign it and it moves, assume that the crystal knows best.

Form: The Flower of Life grows from the Vesica Piscis (see page 52) through six-fold symmetry, which means that the pattern replicates itself equally around its central point with six axes that remain constant, regardless of how many times the grid is expanded. The pattern is the same when viewed from all angles, and the energetic effect is three dimensional. Multiple overlapping circles, each of the same diameter, create a flower-like pattern. The center of each circle is located on the circumference of one of the surrounding circles. Nineteen overlapping circles create thirteen arcs around the edge of an unboundaried Flower. But many other grid shapes (see pages 12 to 14) lie within the Flower, too. The Seed of Life lies at its heart and can be used as a stand-alone grid. Its seven overlapping circles create a flower-like pattern that is beautiful in its simplicity. An outer circle forms a protective barrier to negativity and invasion by outside forces, while the inner circle represents conception, in which the sperm and ova merge before splitting into individual cells. Six cells cluster around the central core to create new life, a feature also found in the Fruit of Life grid (see page 168).

Uses: The Flower of Life or the Seed of Life are particularly potent for manifestation grids that bring goals and desires to a successful conclusion, or for a protective grid to enhance the energies within an area. The grid can also be used to balance the chakras of the physical body and the energy vortex points within the immediate or wider environment for earth healing. It is also a useful focus for meditation and for sending distant healing to other parts of the world either for an individual's needs or for a public situation such as war, famine, or natural disasters.

NOTE:

See pages 162 and 164 for examples of grids based on the Flower of Life.

Timing: You can lay the Flower of Life grid at any time, but it can be extremely effective when laid under the full moon. The Seed of Life is particularly potent when it's set out at a new moon or in the spring.

Amethyst, Danburite, Herkimer Diamond, and Smoky Quartz radiate calming energy and universal love out into the environment in Flower of Life.

Unboundaried Flower of Life

Boundaried Flower of Life

The Seed of Life

Energetic effect.
The Flower of Life replicates and radiates
harmonious energy equally in all directions,
but the flow can be controlled by the crystal
pattern superimposed on it, according to
the intention of the grid.

YOU WILL NEED:

- Template
- Cleansed and empowered crystals according to the grid shape you wish to lay within the Flower
- Sufficient crystals for the outer circle, if creating a boundaried grid
- Keystone to activate the grid

TO LAY THE GRID:

1. If you are laying the complete Flower of Life or the Seed of Life inner grid, you will need a template to follow, because precise positioning is important. Lay the template on a colored background or a material appropriate for your purpose (see pages 20 to 21).
2. Hold your crystals in your hands and state your intention for the grid.
3. Place the keystone in the center of the grid to anchor it.
4. With focused attention, lay a crystal in the center of each flower shape.
5. Lay crystals radiating along the petals of each flower or along the arcs, according to what pleases your inner eye. Trust your intuition.
6. Lay the outer circle with protective crystals, if you're creating a boundaried grid.
7. To activate the grid, gaze at it through softly focused eyes until the energy lights up the grid. (If you're not an experienced practitioner, this may be something you sense or intuit rather than see with your physical eyes.)
8. To dismantle the grid, remove the keystone, and then remove the crystals in the reverse order in which you laid them. The space in which the grid was laid will almost certainly require sound or a clearing essence (see page 29) to completely dismantle it since its energetic imprint is long lasting.

Grid-kit suggestions: Chakra crystals (see page 44), Quartz, Herkimer Diamond, Rose Quartz, Rhodochrosite, Smoky Quartz, Blue Kyanite, Imperial Topaz, Rhodozite

TREE OF LIFE

Kabalistic Tree of Life

Celtic Tree of Life

THE NATURE OF THE DIVINE

The Tree of Life is used in Kabala, the ancient, mystical Jewish practice, to understand the nature of the divine and the way in which the world was created. Depicting the descent of spirit into matter, it is regarded by practitioners as a "map of reality," each of thirty-two pathways leading to an expansion of the knowledge of the divine or the wisdom of the universal mind. In certain approaches, it is the path to knowing God or the Eternal; in others, it is the path to knowing the Self. The Celtic Tree of Life is drawn with the branches reaching skyward and the roots spreading into the earth below, but the branches and roots link in a circle, symbolizing the Druidic belief in the connection between heaven and earth and the eternal nature of cyclic life and afterlife.

Form: The Tree of Life arises from of the center of the Flower of Life (see page 15). Or, in the Celtic approach, it is drawn as a tree with the roots placed deep in the Earth and the branches reaching up to heaven, united by the tree's trunk. In some Celtic forms, the branches and the roots also meet (see left). The Tree of Life can be stretched and expanded to cover the human body (see page 126) or an area within the environment.

Uses: In gridwork, crystals are placed on ten major points of the Kabalistic Tree to bring about integration, since the Tree of Life is used for grids that balance heaven and earth, or that lead to a deeper spiritual understanding. The Kabalistic Tree of Life is particularly useful for laying on and around the body to balance the chakras and energy flow around the body (see page 126). It can also be buried or laid in the external environment, where it can be left in place for long periods of time. The Celtic Tree of Life is the perfect grid for placing in the home to heal the ancestral line (see page 176) and for taking forgiveness back into the past—but it requires a cloth or baseplate on which the tree is printed to place the crystals to maximum effect.

Timing: The Tree of Life can be laid at any time, but the Celtic Tree is particularly effective when adjusted to the cycles and seasons of the year by changing the crystals at the solstices and equinoxes.

YOU WILL NEED:

- Appropriate template and background
- Keystone and anchor stones
  For the Kabalistic Tree: 10 appropriate crystals
  For the Celtic Tree: A selection of light-bringing, grounding, and detoxifying crystals (see page 30)

NOTE:
To lay the Kabalistic grid for chakra balancing, see page 126. To lay the Celtic Tree for ancestral healing, see page 176.

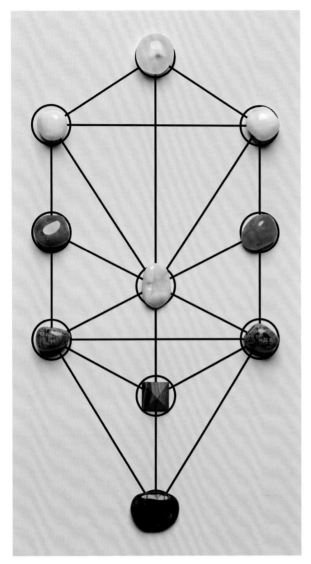

A polished Shungite anchor stone below a Malachite pyramid, African Turquoises, Blue Lace Agate keystone, Orange Carnelians, Rose Quartzes, and Selenite light-bringer cleanse the chakras and enhance the flow of spiritual energy around the body.

TO LAY THE GRID:

1. Select your template and background color according to your intention.
2. Hold your crystals in your hands and state your intention for the grid.
3. If you are laying the Kabalistic Tree to expand your awareness, begin by placing an anchor stone at the base, and then work your way up the tree, using appropriate crystals. Place your anchor stone at the central point of the grid (three circles up from the base).
4. If you are laying the Kabalistic Tree to draw divine energy down into matter, begin by placing the keystone at the topmost circle and then proceed down to the base, where you'll lay the anchor stone.
5. Join the crystals with a crystal wand or the power of your mind.
6. To dismantle the grid, remove the keystone, and then remove the crystals in the reverse order in which you laid them. The space in which the grid was laid will almost certainly require sound or a clearing essence (see page 29) to completely dismantle it since its energetic imprint is long lasting.

Grid-kit suggestions: Ancestralite, Kambaba Jasper, Celtic Quartz, Cradle of Life (Humankind), Freedom Stone, Hematite, Dumortierite, Anandalite™, Selenite, Yellow Calcite, Green Calcite, Clear Calcite

METATRON'S CUBE

THE MAP OF THE MULTIVERSE

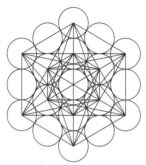

Metatron's Cube

Metatron's Cube is a complex, multi-dimensional connector—that is, it energetically links together all dimensions—arising from the Flower of Life and the Fruit of Life. It plots the four cardinal directions (north, south, east, and west), plus "above," or the divine, and "below," or the Earth. The Cube was used by the alchemists of old as a vehicle for creation—or for containment. It is said to be a map of creation, plotting the "Big Bang" and the ever-unfolding energy that rippled out from that event. But, rather than being a map of a single universe, it is a map of the multiverse: the finite and infinite possible universes, including the universe in which we live and the natural and supernatural worlds. This notion of a multiverse expands space-time and goes right down to the quantum level of creation, so this is the perfect grid for experienced crystal and lightworkers to use to explore all the facets of consciousness and the quantum world that is both everywhere and nowhere at once. It assists in moving us beyond the bounds of everyday, consensual reality into the true nature of that which actually exists beyond our present limited awareness—that is, into the infinite. It is also ideal if you aren't sure of your divine (or earthly) purpose, and need to identify your role in life.

Form: Thirteen equal circles with radiating and interconnecting lines create a one-dimensional picture of Metatron's Cube, but energetically speaking, it's much more powerful than that. This is a pulsating, multi-dimensional maelstrom that benefits from anchor stones placed on the outer circles to keep the energy grounded and contained so that it functions here on Earth. The circles represent feminine energy; the straight lines, masculine energy. The configuration also represents the five fundamental elements: fire, earth, air, metal, and wood. Ultimately, this grid, which contains all of the Platonic solids, is a combination of the forces that hold the universe in balance.

Uses: Named for the archangel Metatron, who facilitates communication between the human and angelic realms, this is a grid of co-creation, inspiration, and transformation. It's perfect for when you need to call on angelic assistance. For instance, it will assist in bringing a guardian angel to you when you feel lost or in need of comfort, or when you require protection. It can also assist with your spiritual development: The angelic being will act as your guide and mentor. The grid can also be used when you wish to replace a negative thought or pattern with a positive one.

One of the Cube's major functions is to facilitate the exploration of the vastness of consciousness and creation. Lay it and meditate on it quietly, allowing your eye and your mind to be drawn through its layers, guided by your higher self. Note how the individual shapes become visible, then recede back into the whole. Metatron's traditional colors are violet, pink, and dark green, but you can choose your crystal colors to correspond to the archangel of your choice (see page 153).

NOTE:
See page 142 to discover another use for this grid.

Timing: Use the Cube whenever it is needed. However, it is a particularly potent tool when it's laid at the winter solstice or the New Year.

Malachite and Rose Quartz around a central clear Quartz keystone call in the assistance of archangel Metatron.

YOU WILL NEED:

- Appropriate template and colored background
- 6 cleansed and empowered crystals
- Keystone
- 6 anchor stones

TO LAY THE GRID:

1. Choose a location in which the grid can remain in place without being disturbed. If you are working with angelic connection, a home altar is ideal.
2. Lay the template on the colored background or a material appropriate for your purpose.
3. Hold your crystals in your hands and state your intention for the grid.
4. Place the six inner circle crystals first.
5. Then place the six outer-circle anchor stones. (If you are replacing a negative thought or pattern, use light-bringing stones for the inner circle and detoxifying stones for the outer circle.)
6. Place the keystone in the center and restate your intention.
7. Meditate quietly with softly focused, half-closed eyes until the grid is activated. (You'll be able to sense the shift in energy when the grid is activated. Some people feel it at a subtle level; others may notice a strong physical sensation, like a sort of "fizzing" in the body; while still others feel their bodies "jump" when activation occurs.)
8. Use a wand or the power of your mind to trace all the connecting lines of the grid. (If you are replacing a negative thought, bring to your mind the positive thought or pattern that will replace it. Ensure that your new thought or intention is phrased in the present tense, not in the future tense. For instance, if your intention is to replace negative body-image thoughts, you might say, "I embrace my strong, healthy, lively body.")
9. To dismantle the grid, remove the keystone, and then remove the crystals in the reverse order in which you laid them. The space in which the grid was laid will almost certainly require sound or a clearing essence (see page 29) to completely dismantle it since its energetic imprint is long lasting.

Grid-kit suggestions: Clearing and light-bringing crystals (see page 30), Anandalite™, Amazez, Auralite 23, Vera Cruz Amethyst, Angel Aura Quartz, Angel's Wing Calcite, Angelite, Celestite, Larimar, Flint, Rutilated Quartz, Petalite, Smoky Quartz, Selenite. See also the archangel crystals on page 153.

CRYSTAL GLOSSARY

MALACHITE

Malachite is a power stone for intense inner transformation and soul catharsis. This crystal is merciless in exposing personality imperfections, outgrown patterns, blockages, and ties that must be dissolved before you can evolve spiritually. It requires you to take responsibility for your thoughts, feelings, and actions. This makes it an excellent karmic and soul cleanser, activating your soul's purpose.

ROSE QUARTZ

Rose Quartz heals emotions and transforms relationships with yourself and others, drawing in love and harmony. This crystal of auric and heart protection brings loving vibes into your heart and subtle etheric bodies. At a metaphysical level, Rose Quartz stimulates the third eye, strengthening scrying power and opening clairvoyance to the finest levels of guidance.

AURALITE 23

This extremely high vibration, multi-layered crystal brings profound peace and clarity, containing as it does the wisdom of the ages.

ANANDALITE™

An exceedingly high vibration crystal, Anandalite draws down cosmic wisdom and connects to celestial beings and the archangels.

MERKABA (STAR TETRAHEDRON)

THE VEHICLE OF LIGHT

The Merkaba is a tool for personal spiritual evolution, raising the frequency of the human body to access Source energy—the energy that underlies all creation. It is an ancient symbol, and its name is derived from the Hebrew word *Merkava*, meaning "chariot." In the Old Testament, it was the vehicle through which the throne of God could be reached. Today, the Merkaba is used to restructure the human energy body so that a higher frequency can flow through it, but it has always been seen as enhancing the flow of *Chi* (life force). Traditionally, the Merkaba is used for protection and cell regeneration. Symbolizing fusion, unity, and perfect harmony, it unites the right and left hemispheres of the brain, stimulating the pineal gland (which is linked to the "third eye" or the "inner eye"). At the material level, the Merkaba creates a balanced mind and a peaceful life. It assists in the manifestation of Love in all its forms.

Form: The Merkaba is a regular three-dimensional polygon constructed from eight equilateral triangular pyramids (tetrahedrons): four pyramids surround the two central core pyramids. The pyramid pointing upward connects to "above," or universal energy, and is yang, positive or masculine energy flow. The pyramid pointing downward connects to the Earth and is yin, negative or feminine energy flow. Energy from each pyramid spins in opposing directions, creating spirals of energy around the body.

Uses: The Merkaba is a tool for ascension, that is, raising the vibration of the human energy field or that of the planet. Use the Merkaba grid to induce deep meditative or trance states. It can create a high-frequency protective shield around the spiritual body, which helps induce and maintain these meditative states, and the protective effect of this shield continues even after you've come out of meditation. The Merkaba aligns and stabilizes the chakras and subtle energy bodies, and it also prevents negative energy in the environment, such as ill-wishing or electromagnetic fields, from reaching the physical body. This is a good grid for addressing sick-building syndrome, for instance.

Timing: No specific timing is required. The Merkaba grid can be used at any time.

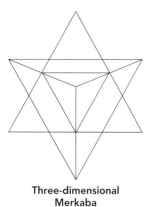

Merkaba

Three-dimensional Merkaba

The energetic effect. The energy spirals around a Merkaba either expand to encompass a space and to act as a bridge between dimensions, or wrap around the whole body, including the energy bodies that surround the physical, penetrating deep into the spaces between the cells and raising the frequency of the body as a whole.

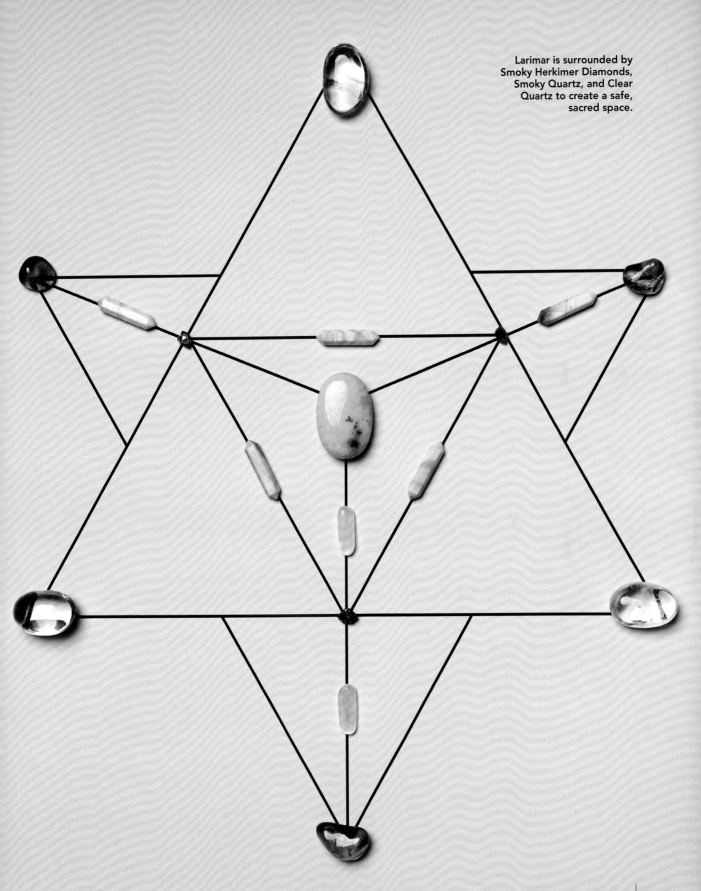

Larimar is surrounded by Smoky Herkimer Diamonds, Smoky Quartz, and Clear Quartz to create a safe, sacred space.

YOU WILL NEED:

- Appropriate template and colored background (see pages 20–21)
- Sufficient light-bringing and grounding crystals to outline the grid
- Keystone
- Crystal wand

TO LAY THE GRID:

1. Select your location. Dowse (see page 31) or use your intuition to do so. Ideally, choose a place where the grid can be left undisturbed, unless you're placing it on or around the body.
2. Lay the template on the colored background, or a material appropriate for your purpose.
3. Hold your crystals in your hands and state your intention for the grid.
4. Outline the largest upward-pointing triangle with light-bringing crystals.
5. Connect the triangle with a crystal wand. (Using a crystal wand—not just the power of your mind—for this grid is ideal, since it'll help keep you focused when creating the shape.)
6. Outline the largest downward-pointing triangle with grounding crystals.
7. Connect the triangle with a crystal wand.
8. Dowse (see page 31) or use your intuition to see which of the connecting lines should be laid with crystals.
9. Place your keystone in the center and state your intention again.
10. Use a crystal wand or the power of your mind to trace the inner triangle and watch the grid light up.
11. If you're using the grid for meditation or metaphysical purposes, look at the grid through softly focused eyes until you can picture it in your mind before closing your eyes.
12. If you're using the grid for environmental enhancement, leave it in place on an altar or other suitable location.
13. To dismantle the grid, remove the keystone, and then remove the crystals in the reverse order in which you laid them. The space in which the grid was laid will almost certainly require sound or a clearing essence (see page 29) to completely dismantle it since its energetic imprint is long lasting.

Grid-kit suggestions: Cleansing and light-bringing crystals (see page 30), Anandalite™, Merkabite Calcite, Blue Kyanite, Fire and Ice Quartz, Labradorite, Trigonic Quartz, Petalite, Danburite, Paraiba Tourmaline, Larimar

CRYSTAL GLOSSARY

SMOKY HERKIMER DIAMOND

Smoky Herkimer is a high-vibration stone and is an excellent psychic clearing tool. It protects against electromagnetic or geopathic pollution and draws its effects out of the subtle bodies.

CLEAR QUARTZ

Clear Quartz works on multi-dimensional levels of being. Generating electromagnetism and dispelling static electricity, it is an extremely powerful healing and energy amplifier.

LARIMAR

Serene Blue Larimar provides freedom from self-imposed limitations and creates a sense of peace through finding truth. It can be used for multi-dimensional and cellular work, and to stimulate the heart and higher chakras.

BLUE KYANITE

Tranquil Blue Kyanite is one of the few crystals that do not hold onto negative energy (but it should nevertheless be cleansed). Its high vibrations rapidly transfer energy and create new energetic and neural pathways, acting like a universal bridge. It opens metaphysical abilities and activates the higher chakras, aligning them with the subtle bodies.

TWELVE-POINTED STAR (DOUBLE MERKABA)

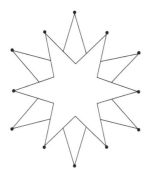

Double star formation

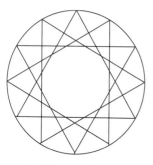

Double Star of David

NOTE:
See page 150 to use the twelve-pointed star for angelic communication.

THE LIGHT-GIVER

In ancient Greece, the twelve-pointed star was a symbol for the life-giving energy of the sun. It links the four elements (earth, air, fire, and water). This elemental flow of energy is a powerful force for activating the pineal gland, awakening higher consciousness, and facilitating communication with higher beings. The star radiates energy across a wide area, but it is also particularly useful for re-energizing ongoing projects that take at least a year to complete—like building a house, writing a book, or training for a marathon.

Form: The twelve-pointed star is configured by laying two hexagram (Star of David) grids, or by creating two superimposed stars at 45-degree angles to each other.

Uses: At its simplest, you can use the twelve-pointed star to fill an area with light and energy, much as you would use a sunburst (see page 68). Placing a crystal on each point, plus a keystone, is all that is required. Use the double Star of David to keep new projects on the move, and to keep their energy turning; they'll be more likely to come to fruition.

Timing: The twelve-pointed star can be laid at any time, but it is particularly potent when laid at the start of a new venture. Begin such ventures in the new year, after the winter solstice, or in the spring—rather than prior to the close of the old year.

YOU WILL NEED:

- Appropriate template and colored background
- 3 activating crystals
- 3 maintaining crystals
- 3 grounding crystals
- 3 red crystals representing fire (spirit)
- 3 smoky crystals representing earth (practicality)
- 3 clear crystals representing air (ideas)
- 3 blue-turquoise crystals representing water (feeling)
- 6 intention crystals
- 3 high-vibration grounding crystals, such as Smoky Herkimer or Elestial Quartz
- Keystone

TO LAY THE GRID:

Stage 1: Planning
First week: Select your location—dowse, use your intuition, or use the bagua on page 34—and place your template where it will remain undisturbed for the duration of the project.

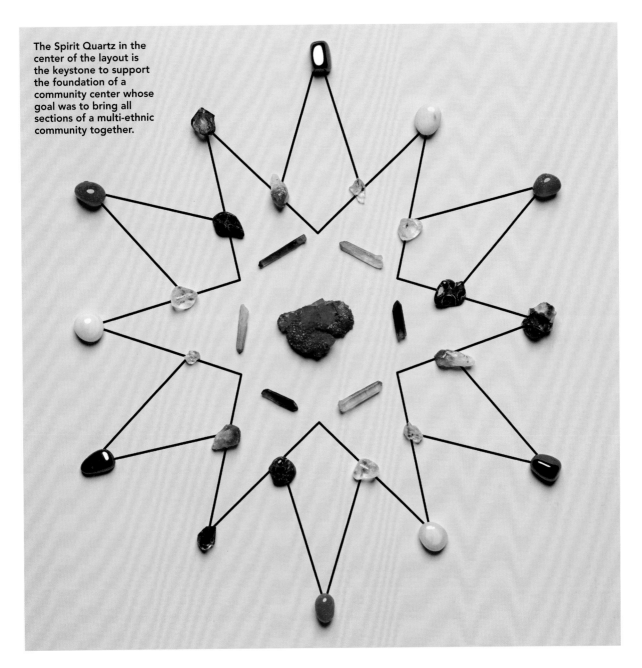

The Spirit Quartz in the center of the layout is the keystone to support the foundation of a community center whose goal was to bring all sections of a multi-ethnic community together.

1. Hold your crystals in your hands and state your intention for the grid.
2. Starting at the left-hand side (ten o'clock position on the template), lay an orange-red crystal on each point of the first large triangle to set the project in motion.
3. Place your keystone in the center to represent the project.

Second week: Move downward, counterclockwise, to the next triangle, and lay a white crystal triangle to keep the grid flowing.

Third week: Move to the next triangle and place a silver or smokey triangle to anchor the energy.

Fourth week: Lay high-vibration ground crystals on the remaining outer points to draw in assistance from higher realms.

Fifth week: Lay an air crystal on the V inside the first triangle point to keep the ideas flowing.

Sixth week: Move to the next triangle point and lay a water crystal on the V inside the triangle point to cleanse the project.

Seventh week: Move to the next triangle point and lay a fire triangle on the V inside the triangle point to keep the momentum going.

Eighth week: Move to the next triangle point and lay an earth triangle on the V inside the triangle point to ground the energies.

Ninth week: Lay six intention stones to form an inner hexagon. around the keystone. Cleanse and rededicate your keystone to fully activate the grid, stating your intention again. This completes the first round of your grid layout. (Adjust your timing if the implementation stage arrives earlier or later than envisaged here.)

Stage 2: Implementation

1. As this stage of the project approaches, cleanse the grid thoroughly and dowse to check whether any crystals need to be replaced. If appropriate, relay and rededicate the grid as above, keeping your keystone in place.

Stage 3: Ongoing

1. As the project is fully manifested, cleanse the grid thoroughly and dowse to check if any crystals need to be replaced. If appropriate, relay and rededicate the grid following the instructions above, keeping your keystone in place.
2. Touch the keystone and state your intention once more.
3. Leave the grid in place until the project is well established or completed.
4. To dismantle the grid, remove the stones in the reverse order in which they were placed, leaving the keystone until last. (There's no need to use sound or clearing essence for dismantling this particular grid. You can happily leave its energy to continue working, even after it's been dismantled.)

Grid-kit suggestions: Elemental crystals (see below), grounding crystals (see page 30), light-bringing crystals (see page 30), intention crystals (see page 30), archangel crystals (see page 153)

ELEMENTAL CRYSTALS

Earth: Smoky Quartz, Shungite, Black Tourmaline, Agate, Jasper, Flint, Territulla Agate
Air: Amethyst, Moldavite, Tektite, Sapphire, Blue Chalcedony, Picture Jasper
Fire: Fire Agate, Obsidian, Triplite, Carnelian, Citrine, Rubellite, Sunstone
Water: Aquamarine, Calcite, Blue Lace Agate, Moonstone, Blue Tourmaline

CRYSTAL GLOSSARY

BLACK TOURMALINE (EARTH)

Most Black Tourmaline contains iron, making it a powerfully protective stone. Due to its inner structure, however, Tourmaline traps negative energy within it rather than bouncing it back and forth as iron-based stones are prone to do. Use it in a grid around your home to create a protective shield that blocks negativity or toxic energy of any kind.

AMETHYST (AIR)

Amethyst opens your third eye and clarifies spiritual vision. By creating a safe sacred space for meditation and multi-dimensional exploration, it clears your mind and aids enlightenment. By detaching you from unwanted entities, thought forms, or mental constructs, Amethyst dispels illusions that prevent you from experiencing true reality. It helps you dream a new world into being.

FIRE AGATE (FIRE)

Fire Agate facilitates the evolution of consciousness. It clears etheric blockages and energizes the aura. Fire Agate has a deep connection to the earth and its energy is calming, bringing security and safety.

AQUAMARINE (WATER)

Aquamarine assists in letting go of mental constructs and underlying emotional states. It reminds you that progress is the law of life—the soul must evolve along the pathway it laid down for itself prior to incarnation.

INFINITE HEXAGRAM

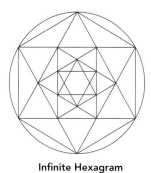

Infinite Hexagram

THE UNFOLDING UNIVERSE

The Infinite Hexagram represents both the balance of celestial forces with terrestrial ones *and* a portal to other worlds. It can be expanded or contracted infinitely as required, and it symbolizes ultimate harmony and expansion, neatly contained within its outer limits. A powerful force for transformation and change, this potent grid can balance your energies and encourage rejuvenation of mind, body, and spirit if you lie within it. The process for laying the grid is the same, whether you're placing it on and around the body or on or in a physical space. But the energetic effects extend way beyond any given physical space, shifting vibrations and energy frequencies to a higher level. The Infinite Hexagram can also be used to (safely) access multi-dimensions of consciousness and the Akashic record.

Form: The six points of the inner hexagram become the starting point for each succeeding hexagon and hexagram that expands out from it, the points of the hexagram being joined within a hexagon and then extended. It is a threefold opening-out, for each new hexagram is three times the size of the previous one.

Uses: Use the Infinite Hexagram if you want to kick-start change and transformation, and then to restructure the energies to accommodate that change. You could, for instance, lay the Infinite Hexagram if you want to identify your true vocation and find the means of support while you retrain, if necessary.

Timing: Use the Infinite Hexagram whenever you want to bring about orderly change or restore order to a chaotic situation. It is an excellent grid to lay at spring or a new moon to set things in motion. Refresh the grid at the quarter and full moons, or at the equinoxes and solstices.

NOTE:
See pages 158–159 for a Sri Yantra variation on the Infinite Hexagram that accesses the Akashic past lives.

Keystone: Orange Sphalerite to assist the physical body to assimilate an energetic shift. Inner hexagram incorporates Hematite and Chrysotile to clear karmic factors. Lapis Lazuli on the next hexagram stabilizes the new energies. Outer hexagram uses Chrysotile and Clear Quartz to bring further clarification and restructuring.

YOU WILL NEED:

- A template and appropriate colored background—ideally, a background with the template printed on it
- Sufficient crystals to place at each line intersection if appropriate, either a mixture of crystal types or crystals of the same type
- Keystone for the center
- Anchor stones for the perimeter if appropriate. (Dowse, see page 31, or use your intuition to ascertain how many and what type.)

TO LAY THE GRID:

1. Hold your crystals in your hands and state your intention for the grid.
2. Place crystals on the three points of the inner downward-pointing triangle to anchor the energies.
3. Place crystals on the three points of the inner upward-pointing triangle to draw energy in.
4. With your crystal wand or the power of your mind, connect the points to make a hexagon around the outer edges of the two triangles.
5. Extend the hexagon into a hexagram by further placing crystals to create the points of the next hexagram.
6. Repeat until you have reached the appropriate number of hexagrams.
7. Place your keystone in the center and restate your intention.
8. Lay anchor stones around the perimeter if appropriate.
9. To dismantle the grid, remove the keystone, and then remove the crystals in the reverse order in which you laid them. The space in which the grid was laid will almost certainly require sound or a clearing essence (see page 29) to completely dismantle it since its energetic imprint is long lasting.

Grid-kit suggestions: Anandalite™, Trigonic Quartz, Lemurian Seed, Moldavite, Tektite, Flint, Libyan Gold Tektite, Rainbow Mayanite, Chrysotile, Lapis Lazuli

CRYSTAL GLOSSARY

LAPIS LAZULI

Lapis Lazuli is a key to spiritual attainment. Enhancing dreamwork and metaphysical abilities, it facilitates spiritual journeying and stimulates personal and spiritual power. By transmuting mental and emotional blockages, Lapis sets your soul free to express itself fully.

HEMATITE

Useful for past-life healings that involve war, wounds, and bloodshed, this powerful stone also assists in overcoming addictions rooted in emotional cravings or unfulfilled desires. Hold Hematite to ground the soul back into your body after journeying or spiritual work.

CHRYSOTILE

Chrysotile links you to the knowledge of the ages. This stone helps you to clear away the debris of the past to reveal your core Self. It also works on the etheric blueprint to correct imbalances and blockages that could manifest as disease. Toxic—always use tumbled.

MOLDAVITE

A meteorite flew in from outer space and fused with the ground on which it landed, uniting heaven and earth to create Moldavite. This high-vibration crystal links "above" and "below," accessing the Akashic record and All That Is (source energy).

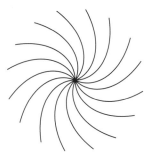

Multi-armed spiral

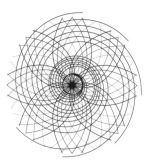

Energetic effect. A multi-armed spiral creates an energetic vortex that either spirals energy out into the environment to re-energize it, or sucks energy into its center to transmute it.

NOTE:

If you are laying the grid on and around your physical body, ask a friend to assist. Dowse (see page 31) or use your intuition to find out where to place the keystone and how the spiral arms should be extended over your body and out into your subtle bodies, placing the crystals on and around your physical body as you do so.

MULTI-ARMED SPIRAL

COSMIC CONSCIOUSNESS

The multi-armed spiral represents cosmic consciousness and the forces that hold the universe together spiraling around the central womb of creation. It is laid in much the same way as a single spiral or a sunburst, but it generates and radiates energy over a much wider area, creating an unfolding energy vortex that is surprisingly stable. It will also generate and draw in energy where required. It is particularly useful for reviving an energetically "dead" area—such as a patch of earth, a house, a room, or even a desk—and can be placed on maps or the environment for earth-healing. This is a reflective grid, for spiral galaxies are found both in the outer reaches of space and within the whirlpools and eddies of the smallest puddle.

Form: Spiral, curved arms radiate with perfect symmetry, joining together at the center.

Uses: Lay this grid whenever intense activation, energization, and rejuvenation are required—for instance, when you move into a new house, after a relationship has finished, or when you feel like you've become "stuck" with a creative project. Lay it over a chakra or the dantien, or in the environment. You can also lay the grid as a meditation or journeying focus.

Timing: Lay your multi-armed spiral at any time, but it is particularly effective when laid at the solstices and equinoxes to keep the energies of the Earth revitalized and replenished.

YOU WILL NEED:

- An appropriate place to lay your grid, depending on its size and where it's to be placed—such as a patch of earth or floor, or a base made of a natural surface that will ground the energy, such as petrified wood, slate, or marble
- Sufficient crystals to lay the arms of the spiral
- Keystone for the center and anchor stones

TO LAY THE GRID:

1. Hold your crystals in your hands and state your intention for the grid.
2. Lay your keystone at the center.
3. If you're laying the grid to radiate energy, lay crystals along each of the arms, beginning at the center. If you're using the grid to activate your chakras or draw power into your dantien, reverse the direction of flow by placing the crystals at the end of the spiral arms first, then working in toward the keystone.
4. Use a crystal wand or the power of your mind to activate the grid.
5. If appropriate, lay an anchor stone alongside the grid.
6. To dismantle the grid, remove the crystals in the reverse order in which you laid them, leaving the keystone for last. (There's no need to use sound or clearing essence for dismantling this particular grid. You can happily leave its energy to continue working, even after it's been dismantled.)

Flint cleanses and transmutes toxic energies. Celtic Golden Healer and Celtic Chevron Quartz radiate healing and stability into the environment.

Grid-kit suggestions: Anandalite™, Moldavite, Selenite, Rhodozite, Celtic Healer Quartz, Golden Quartz, Flint, Black Tourmaline, Hematite, Smoky Quartz

TRIPLE SPIRAL (THE TRISKELION)

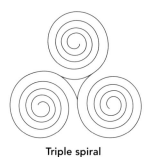

Triple spiral

LIFE CYCLES

The triple spiral is a dynamic symbol of activation, movement, and expansion, in contrast to all that is fixed and firm. It is a cyclical grid, symbolizing life moving forward. It represents the three faces of the moon (new, full, and dark); the three phases of life (conception, birth, and death); as well as other triads, like the creation, sustenance, and destruction of life. And it presents the three faces of female power: maiden, mother, and crone. The triple spiral contains extremely ancient astronomical knowledge, the meaning of which has largely been lost. It is found on monuments throughout the Celtic world, but it can also be glimpsed in petroglyphs all around the globe.

Form: Three equal-sized interlocked spirals create the triple spiral. It brings together opposing forces, harmonizing and releasing them through the upper spiral—or draws energy down from the top spiral to infuse the bottom two.

Uses: Use the triple spiral if you need to draw dynamic energy into a situation or to infuse it with light. It is the perfect grid to help you move through life's transition phases, marking rites such as puberty and menopause (which literally translates as the "moon of pause"). This grid can also become a meditation pathway to expanded consciousness. Use tiny crystals to lay the triple spiral over the third eye and soma chakras to open your inner sight.

The triple spiral layout not only highlights and heals the present situation but also reveals its origins. The bottom right hand spiral represents the present situation. The left hand spiral signifies the underlying causes behind the situation. The top spiral ensures a beneficial outcome as you move into the next cycle. It can be used for the family, in work or friendship situations, or for the benefit of the wider world.

Timing: Lay the grid at any time; however, it is particularly effective when laid in three stages at the dark, new, and full moons to create ritual space or to facilitate transition.

An Eye of the Storm (Judy's Jasper) Merkaba is the keystone for the grid. The top spiral is Turquoise to clarify communication. The left-hand spiral is Smoky Quartz to cleanse the energies, and the right-hand spiral is Citrine to infuse bright energy into the resolution of the situation.

YOU WILL NEED:

- Template and appropriate background
- Sufficient crystals to complete the spirals
- Keystone

TO LAY THE GRID:

1. Hold your crystals in your hands and state your intention for the grid.
2. Begin with the center stone of the upper spiral, then lay that spiral.
3. Use the power of your mind or a crystal wand to activate the spiral, taking the energy from the center to the edge.
4. When the timing is right (that is, when you see a change beginning to occur in the situation, when your intuition tells you it is time, or when the moon changes phase), continue into the next spiral and join the two.
5. When the timing is right, continue into the third spiral and join at the center.
6. Use a crystal wand or the power of your mind to connect the three spirals once again. (The easiest way to do this is to use the spaces between the lines of crystals, making your way to the heart of the configuration.)
7. Place your keystone in the center of the triple spiral and restate your intention.
8. To dismantle the grid, remove the crystals in the reverse order in which you laid them, leaving the keystone for last. (There's no need to use sound or clearing essence for dismantling this particular grid. You can happily leave its energy to continue working, even after it's been dismantled.)

NOTE:
See page 178 to discover how to use the triple spiral for situational healing.

Grid-kit suggestions: Ancestralite, Freedom Stone, Cradle of Life (Humankind), Celtic Healer Quartz, Menalite, Quartz, Rose Quartz, Citrine, Turquoise, Smoky Quartz, and see page 178

CRYSTAL GLOSSARY

TURQUOISE

Turquoise lets you explore past lives to find the primary source of a martyred attitude or self-sabotage. If you are pessimistic, it teaches you to focus on solutions rather than problems or the past. This stone dispels negative belief patterns and removes toxic energy, reminding you that you are a spiritual being who happens to be having a human learning experience.

EYE OF THE STORM (JUDY'S JASPER)

Eye of the Storm gives you core stability in which to calmly ride out changes and challenges. It reminds you that the bigger picture is ever changing, offering an objective perspective on how your actions could affect the outcome. This stone instills a deep sense of self-worth from which to interact with the outside world.

MENALITE

The perfect stone to accompany all of the transitions of womanhood, Menalite is excellent for stimulating conception and assisting birth in all its forms. It maintains hormonal balance and removes fear of death.

CRADLE OF LIFE (HUMANKIND)

Rock from the cave where the first human ancestral bones were discovered, Cradle of Life takes you back to first principles and root causes. It rebuilds your sense of self, inputting new, more appropriate patterns.

THE DRAGON'S EYE (TETRAHEDRON)

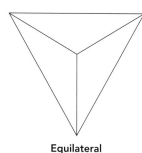

Equilateral Dragon's Eye

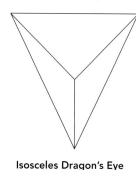

Isosceles Dragon's Eye

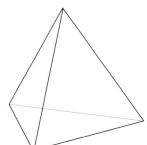

Three-sided pyramid

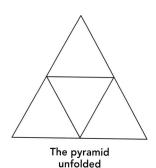

The pyramid unfolded

THE ALL-SEEING EYE

Drawing on the power of triangles, the Dragon's Eye is a potent symbol of protection. This grid creates balance and grounds energy. It also opens the third eye: the metaphysical, all-seeing "eye of insight" located in the center of the forehead. It integrates inner and outer, and higher and lower, vibrations. The Dragon's Eye helps you to see the treasure lying within you. It facilitates the release of the fears and ingrained emotional blockages that have to be overcome before you recognize your true self, and it helps you to recognize the beauty and mystery that is all around you. This is the perfect layout for attracting a guardian spirit, especially a dragon mentor (see page 154).

Form: The Dragon's Eye is a downward-pointing equilateral triangle (in which all angles and sides are equal), or an isosceles triangle (in which two angles and sides are equal), with a Y in the middle connecting the three points of the triangle. In its three-dimensional form, the Dragon's Eye creates a three-sided tetrahedron pyramid with four triangular faces, six straight edges, and four vertex corners.

Uses: Call on the Dragon's Eye for protection in your day-to-day life, when you're walking down a dark street, for instance, or in your spiritual life, when you're undertaking a shamanic journey, perhaps. It can also help to open your metaphysical abilities. Use it to infuse love and wisdom into power; to facilitate the transition between the maiden, mother, and crone phases of life; or to unite earth, sea, and sky. Any objective that requires balance and unity between three points responds well to the Dragon's Eye.

Timing: Use whenever protection is required. To open the inner eye—your intuition—lay it at a new moon.

YOU WILL NEED:

- Sufficient crystals for the outer rim, the upper V, and the stem of the Y
- Keystone according to the intention of the layout

TO LAY THE GRID:

1. Hold your crystals in your hands and state your intention for the grid.
2. Place appropriate crystals around the outer triangle.
3. Place appropriate crystals on the upper arms of the Y to form a V-shape, leaving a space in the center.
4. Place appropriate crystals on the tail of the Y.
5. Place your keystone at the center of the Y.
6. Join up the grid with a crystal wand or the power of your mind to activate it. Begin with the outer triangle and then form the Y, taking the energy from the circle toward the central keystone to anchor the energies. (This creates a circular zigzag vibrational force.)

Blue Kyanite and
Hematite open
and ground the
all-seeing eye.

7. If the grid is laid on your forehead, close your eyes and draw your attention to the point above and between your eyebrows. Ask that your inner eye be opened. You may feel tingling and see spirals of intense color, or an actual eye looking at you on your inner "screen."

8. If the grid is laid in front of you, gaze at it with softly focused eyes, asking that your inner sight be activated. (If you feel it's appropriate, lean over the grid and place your third eye on the keystone. Breathe deeply, imagining the energy penetrating deep into your brow to open the third eye.)

9. To dismantle the grid, follow the instructions on page 39. (There's no need to use sound or clearing essence for dismantling this particular grid. You can happily leave its energy to continue working, even after it's been dismantled.)

Grid-kit suggestions: Kyanite, Herkimer Diamond, Rhodozite, Apophyllite, Smoky Quartz, and see protective crystals (page 30) and intuitive crystals (page 30)

NOTE:
See page 154 to discover how to use the grid or to call in a dragon mentor.

THE LABYRINTH

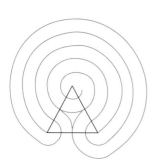

THE INNER SELF

The Labyrinth is a journey of discovery into your deepest Self through the passage of time, and it encompasses change, growth, progress, and transformation. When you walk the sacred Labyrinth, you walk into your inner core. The journey takes you into wholeness and centeredness, helping you to be grounded around that core. The Labyrinth continually expands your vision of what is possible for you, and what your soul intended for you on your pathway through life. It helps you to see clearly and to listen deeply. The pattern also represents the two poles of the body and the circulation of vital energies around them: "above" lie the convolutions of the brain, and "below" are the coiled intestines. (This means that the Labyrinth can also be useful for abdominal healing.) It is particularly appropriate for laying in the environment, where it can be left alone to do its work or traversed as a meditation practice.

Form: The Labyrinth is one of the oldest grids in existence. It takes many forms, but all share the core design—a winding pathway leading from the outer edge to the center. Unlike a maze, a Labyrinth has no dead ends or blind alleys. Although it twists and turns, it ultimately leads to the central point, and then out again. Since it is built on an equilateral triangle, the Labyrinth has sacred geometry at its heart.

Uses: A Labyrinth harmonizes the two sides of the brain, bringing together intuition and logic. Walk the Labyrinth to answer a question or to bring insight. Simply focus on the question as you begin to lay the crystals. Also, walking the Labyrinth with a quiet mind brings you into a meditative state, in which you can focus on one of its symbolic meanings as a seed-thought from which deeper insight grows. These symbolic meanings include the spiritual path; wholeness; the passage of time; connection to Source; enlightenment and evolution; rebirth and resurrection; the emergence of the new from the old; and spiritual growth.

Timing: Lay a Labyrinth at a new moon, if you're taking a journey into yourself. Lay it at a full moon to harmonize the different sides of the brain, to gain insight, or to ask a question.

Smoky Quartz and Turquoise lead the soul into the center of the Labyrinth to meet the vibrant spirit energy of a Herkimer Diamond.

YOU WILL NEED:

- Chalk or spray paint if constructing an outdoor Labyrinth; template for an indoor layout
- Sufficient crystals to lay along the lines of the whole Labyrinth
- Keystone for the center

Note: If you are laying a permanent Labyrinth in the environment, choose sturdy crystals that won't dissolve in wet conditions.

TO LAY THE GRID:

1. If you're setting your Labyrinth in the environment, draw it out with chalk or spray paint first. Otherwise, place the template in a location where it will not be disturbed.
2. Hold your crystals in your hands and state your intention for the grid.
3. Begin at the Labyrinth's entrance point. If you're in the environment, lay the stones on the lines as you walk between them. If you're creating a smaller grid and are "walking" with your finger, place suitably sized crystals to allow your passage to the Labyrinth's center.
4. Place the keystone at the center of the grid and state your intention once more.
5. Walk out carefully so that you do not disturb the stones.
6. To dismantle the grid, follow the instructions on page 39. (There's no need to use sound or clearing essence for dismantling this particular grid. You can happily leave its energy to continue working, even after it's been dismantled.)

Grid-kit suggestions:
Outdoor grids: Clear, Milk, Smoky, Celtic or Rose Quartz; Granite; Basalt; Hematite
Insight grids: Ammonite, Ammolite, Petalite, Obsidian, Malachite, Selenite, Kyanite, Quartz, Bytownite, Labradorite, Azurite, Trigonic Quartz

To Construct a Simple Labyrinth in the Environment

CHAPTER SIX

SPECIFIC GRIDS

THE SPECIFIC EXAMPLE GRIDS included in this section have been successfully used to assist in personal, environmental, or healing-related situations. They're intended to inspire you to begin your own grid creation. You can adapt the crystals within the grids to suit your own individual needs or adapt the grid templates themselves in accordance with what your intuition feels is right for you. Several of the grids in this section have been adapted from basic templates, as you will see. Dowse (see page 31) or use your intuition to find which crystals are appropriate, especially when you're creating mood-altering grids. You'll find suggestions for this in the grid-kits, but please don't limit yourself to these. Be creative and inspired!

SPECIFIC GRIDS

PERSONAL

HOME AND ENVIRONMENT

DISTANCE HEALING

EARTH HEALING

GROUNDING

Layout: Inverted "Golden Triangle"

Many people find it difficult to anchor themselves on the planet. Impractical and disconnected, they "live in their heads," so to speak, or exist mainly in their imaginations, frequently spending most of their time in the past, or in the future, rather than the here and now. But this grid can help. Grounding guides you to settle yourself in the present moment and to actualize your intentions.

Using the grid: This grid is best laid directly onto and around your body while you are lying on the floor, or in the environment. But you can also lay it beneath your bed to anchor you while you sleep.

Timing: This grid can be used at any time. It is particularly important before and after carrying out rituals that connect you to angels and higher beings, like the Angelic layout on page 151. It is also helpful before any kind of spiritual opening-up, meditation, visualization, or even a ritual that doesn't involve crystal grids, as it keeps your energy grounded.

Color and background: Earthy colors such as brown, ochre, or green, or natural materials.

YOU WILL NEED:

- 3 grounding crystals
- 2 Magnesite
- 2 Charoite or Flint

TO LAY THE GRID:

1. Hold your cleansed crystals in your hands and state your intention.
2. Lie down comfortably to get a sense of the space required.
3. Sit up again and place a Smoky Quartz or other grounding crystal below your feet.
4. Place a Charoite or Flint on each knee.
5. Lie down and place a Magnesite on each side of your body in the groin crease.
6. Place a Flint, Smoky Quartz, or other grounding crystal on either side of you, level with your navel.
7. Place your hands on the Magnesite.
8. Use the power of your mind to connect the triangle.
9. With your mind, feel the grid connecting to the Earth star chakra beneath your feet and then to the Gaia gateway chakra and the planet below.
10. Lie still for fifteen minutes, enjoying this connection to Mother Earth.
11. Remove the crystals in the opposite order in which you placed them, placing at least one in your pocket to remind yourself of your experience. Choose whichever crystal resonates with you, and carry it in your pocket for as long as you feel connected to it. When you feel that the crystal has lost its charge, you can repeat the layout.

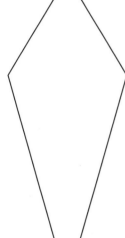

The psoas muscle release layout

Grid-kit suggestions: Brown Carnelian, Charoite, Flint, Hematite, Magnesite, Smoky Quartz, Mookaite Jasper, Polychrome Jasper

EXTENDING THE GRID: THE PSOAS MUSCLE RELAXER

Much of the physical discomfort we experience arises from a tense psoas muscle, which connects the torso with the legs and lower body. Extending the grounding grid—by adding one more crystal to create an equilateral triangle at the top—quickly relaxes this muscle.

TO LAY THE GRID:

1. After placing the grounding crystals at your hips (see step 6 on left and the photograph on the right), add another Smoky Quartz or Flint at the base of your breastbone.
2. Join up the grid with the power of your mind.
3. Breathe gently and easily into the base of your belly, making each out-breath longer than the in-breath.
4. Continue laying the grid by following the instructions of the grounding grid on the left.

The psoas muscle release and grounding layout placed on a young dancer to enhance his flexibility and stamina. Flint, Magnesite, and Smoky Quartz with Charoite on the knees.

INSTANT PROTECTION

**Layout: straight line
in a square**

This layout connects your crown chakra, higher heart chakra (thymus), and earth chakra to ground and transmute detrimental energies and to protect you from harm. Laid within a square, the perimeter prevents negative thoughts and energies from reaching you. An additional crystal worn over your higher heart chakra connects you to the grid during the entire day.

Using the grid: Lay the grid under your bed to protect you during the night and to transmute any detrimental energies you might have picked up during the day. The grid could also be laid in your personal workspace to keep it full of creativity, productivity, and positive energy. To do so, put Carnelian, Red Jasper, and Orange Kyanite inside the corners of the square in addition to the basic crystals.

Timing: Use whenever needed. Leave in place for long periods of time—even for a number of years, as long as it's cleansed regularly.

Color and background: Black and brown stones are the most effective for protection. The grid does not need to be laid on a background; it can be placed directly on the floor.

YOU WILL NEED:

- 3 protective stones (see page 30)
- 4 anchor stones
- Additional stone to be worn as a pendant

TO LAY THE GRID:

1. Hold your crystals in your hands and state your intention for the grid.
2. Place one crystal below where your feet will be when you lie down.
3. Place one crystal where the crown of your head will be.
4. Place one crystal beneath where your higher heart chakra will be (you'll lie on top of this crystal if the grid is beneath your bed, or if you are lying in the grid yourself).
5. Place four anchor crystals in a square around your bed (or workspace).
6. Lie down and breathe quietly within the grid. Feel the energy strengthening your boundaries.
7. Using the power of your mind, connect the straight-line crystals together, and then bring the crystal connection to the pendant in your hand.
8. Connect the square, using the power of your mind.
9. Place the pendant around your neck. Wear it constantly, for as long as you feel connected to it.
10. Remember to cleanse the grid regularly and the pendant daily.

Grid-kit suggestions: Apache Tear, Black Tourmaline, Shungite, Smoky Quartz, Labradorite, Mohawkite, Tantalite, Polychrome Jasper, Porcelain Jasper, Amber, Flint

Shungite and Black Tourmaline are powerful protectors against EMFs.

GENERAL WELL-BEING

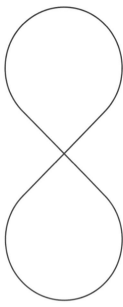

Layout: Lemniscate

The upper and lower loops on a lemniscate layout do not need to be of equal size, and they can be adjusted to fit your body as required. This well-being layout connects your thymus (higher heart chakra), which controls your immune system, with your extended energy body, toning up your overall integrated holistic energy system—that is, your physical, emotional, mental, and spiritual selves—to ensure well-being.

Using the grid: This grid is particularly useful if you suspect you're coming down with a cold or the flu, but use it at any time to support your well-being.

Timing: Use whenever you feel in need of a tone-up of your physical or subtle energies.

Color and background: Blue is a traditional healing color.

YOU WILL NEED:

- 1 clearing crystal
- 1 light-bringing crystal
- 1 immune-balancing crystal

TO LAY THE GRID:

1. Hold your crystals in your hands and state your intention for the grid.
2. Lie down.
3. Place a clearing crystal beneath your feet (sit up to do so).
4. Place a light-bringing crystal above your head.
5. Place an immune-balancing crystal halfway up your breastbone over the higher heart chakra.
6. Use the power of your mind to connect the lemniscate over and around you.
7. Remain in the grid for five to fifteen minutes, focusing your attention and breathing gently into the immune-balancing crystal. If you become aware of energy that needs to shift out of your body, send it down to the crystal at your feet for transmutation.
8. Remove the crystals in the reverse order in which you laid them, then cleanse them according to the instructions on page 39.

Note: The grid can also be laid beneath your bed.

Grid-kit suggestions: *Immune-balancing crystals*: Bloodstone; Green Aventurine; Que Sera (Llanoite); Quantum Quattro; Cherry, Rose, Smoky, or Emerald Quartz. See also cleansing crystals (page 30) and light-bringing crystals (page 30).

Selenite above the head, Bloodstone over the thymus, and an anchor stone at the feet complete the simple lemniscate layout.

RE-ENERGIZING THE BODY

**Layout: Merkaba
(see page 86)**

In today's challenging and stressed-filled world, it is easy to become energetically depleted and suffer burn-out. But a simple grid can quickly recharge your energy. This revitalizing grid also works well to fortify yourself in advance and then allow you to draw on the energy throughout the day. It will lend courage to your convictions and give you the tenacity to see something through. The red-based Merkaba is helpful when you need to recharge your energy after a particularly hectic day but still wish to go out and party in the evening (Red Calcite is excellent for this). Whenever you are feeling listless and apathetic, this is the grid for you. A Merkaba has always been seen as promoting the flow of Qi (life force) around the body. This grid is also helpful for stimulating a flagging libido and bringing passion back into your life. The grid draws on the power of red, an intense color that resonates with the base chakra and which symbolizes passion, vigor, and *joie de vivre*.

Form: The invigorating shape can either be laid on the body around the navel or placed on a table in front of you. The Merkaba grid is formed from six crystals laid in an interlocking hexagram around a central keystone. If the keystone utilizes a combination stone that also grounds the energy, the effect is strengthened, but the grid can also be anchored with grounding stones.

Using the grid: This grid is for short-term use whenever you feel energetically depleted or in need of a sexual reboot. You can also lay it in advance to charge up your energies and store the power for use when required. It is particularly helpful when you have a busy day scheduled and will need to manage your energies so that your vitality stays the course. Whenever you find yourself flagging, take five minutes out to lay the grid and draw the power into your dantien. Then let it flow up your spine. Or, simply tape the keystone into your navel for sustained energy release. Anchor the grid with grounding stones if necessary.

Timing: This energizing grid is the perfect start to your day as it stimulates the flow of Qi. It ensures that you will have energy to spare no matter what life throws at you. It can also replenish your energy any time it dips. Do not use the grid close to bedtime, however, or when feeling angry or frustrated as it could create insomnia or cause your emotions to become volatile and over-heated. Unless, of course, you are looking forward to a night of passion. In which case, lay the grid before retiring.

Merkaba grid to re-energize the body using Coral crystals centered around a Yellow Jasper keystone and anchored with Amazonite hearts.

YOU WILL NEED:

- 6 energizing crystals (see grid-kit suggestions below)
- Keystone
- Anchor stones if appropriate

TO LAY THE GRID:

1. Hold your crystals in your hands and state your intention for the grid.
2. Lay the first triangle, placing a crystal on each point. (If you are laying the grid on your body, place the triangle so that it surrounds your navel.) Join up the triangle with a wand or the power of your mind.
3. Lay an overlocking triangle over the top of the first, pointing in the opposite direction. Join up the points.
4. Place your keystone in the center to create the Merkaba, stating your intention once more. (If you are laying the grid on your body, place the keystone in your navel.)
5. If the grid is in front of you, place your hands over it. As you breathe in, draw the power of the crystals into your hands, up your arms, and down your body to your belly. As you breathe out, consciously hold the crystal power in your belly, circling it in toward your dantien. If the grid is laid on your body, breathe deeply down to the keystone and push the power of the grid down into the dantien just below your navel. As you breathe out, consciously hold the crystal power in your belly, curling it in the dantien.
6. When you're ready to dismantle the grid, gather up the outer stones. Do not cleanse the space. Place the keystone in your hip pocket. Hold it to your dantien whenever you need to draw on the energy. Feel the energy rise up to infuse your whole body, moving into the spaces between your cells as though an electrical charge is passing between them and fizzing through your entire body. Or, tape the keystone in place for slow release. If you are using the grid to stimulate your libido, keep the stone close to you until you are ready to sleep and then place it outside of the room.

Grid-kit suggestions:
Stimulating: Red Garnet, Red Mookaite Jasper, Red Coral*, Ruby, Poppy Jasper, Red Jasper, Fire Agate, Orange River Hematoid Quartz, Bixbite, Red Carnelian, Red Calcite, Harlequin Quartz, Ruby Aura Quartz, Red Amethyst, Cobalto Calcite, Orange Calcite, Sunstone
Grounding: Garnet in Granite or Limestone matrix, Ruby in Kyanite or Zoisite, Poppy Jasper, Amazonite, Green Aventurine, Flint, Yellow Mookaite Jasper

Note: As Coral is an endangered species, ensure that the piece you buy is ethically sourced.

CRYSTAL GLOSSARY

AMAZONITE

Amazonite shields the body from the effects of subtle radiation and electromagnetic frequencies, including WiFi, which depletes the immune systems in sensitive people. The stone also aligns the subtle nervous system with the physical nervous system and relieves muscle spasms.

CORAL

Coral is not a crystal, but it is highly charged with passionate Qi, especially in its red form. It has been a living organism and should be used judiciously. It traditionally assists blood and circulatory system issues and enhances vitality. *Note:* As Coral is an endangered species, ensure that you buy ethically sourced Coral that has not been obtained from a living reef.

MOOKAITE JASPER

Mookaite is an excellent substitute for Coral. This highly potent crystal infuses the body with vitality and either sedates (yellow) or stimulates (red) the immune system as required.

SUNSTONE

Sunstone stimulates vitality and brings the light of the sun into the body and the aura. It is particularly effective for Seasonal affective disorder, and disperses stress and tension. Use it to attract abundance.

EMF CLEARING

Layout: Unicursal hexagram

If you're sensitive to them, electromagnetic fields (EMFs) may have a detrimental effect on your health, so regularly clearing your energy body is both sensible and simple. EMFs are generated by computers, WiFi, cell phones, power lines, electricity-generating stations, "smart-meters," and electrical equipment in general. Airplanes are EMF hotspots, as there is nowhere for the fields to discharge, and trains and cars also contain concentrated fields. EMFs make a significant contribution to sick-building syndrome (see Glossary, page 182).

Using the grid: If you suffer from general malaise and ongoing tiredness, if you feel worse in a particular environment and better when away from it, or if you use your cell phone or computer regularly, spend five minutes in the grid each evening to clear your energy field.

Timing: Daily, or as necessary.

Background and color: Natural materials, like wood or slate, work well for this grid.

YOU WILL NEED:

- 1 light-bringing crystal: Selenite, Amethyst, Herkimer Diamond, or Rose Quartz
- 5 EMF-clearing crystals (see grid-kit suggestions at right)
- 1 Herkimer Diamond or other keystone

TO LAY THE GRID:

1. Hold your crystals in your hands and state your intention for the grid.
2. Lie down comfortably on a bed or the floor.
3. Place a light-bringing crystal over your head.
4. Place an EMF-clearing crystal to your right-hand side, level with your groin.
5. Place an EMF-clearing crystal level with your left ear.
6. Place an EMF-clearing crystal below your feet.
7. Place an EMF-clearing crystal level with your right ear.
8. Place an EMF-clearing crystal on your left-hand side, level with your groin.
9. Place a Herkimer Diamond or other keystone over your higher heart chakra (thymus).
10. Use the power of your mind to activate the grid.

11. Breathe out, consciously allowing the EMF energy to drain down toward the crystal at your feet.

12. Breathe into your belly, drawing energy from the light-bringing crystal down through the grid and into your energy body.

13. Repeat the breaths ten times, and lie within the grid for as long as you feel you need to. Trust your intuition to tell you when to get up.

14. Remove the crystals in the reverse order in which they were laid, then cleanse them according to the instructions on page 39. Unless you live close to a source of EMFs, place crystals in the sun and air to recharge.

Grid-kit suggestions: *EMF-clearing crystals:* Amber, Shungite, Black Tourmaline, Herkimer Diamond, Smoky Quartz, Lepidolite, Green Aventurine, Amethyst, Amber, Cherry and Emerald Quartz, Rose Quartz, Celtic Quartz, Ajoite in Shattukite, Amazonite, Lepidolite. (See *Crystal Prescriptions (Volume 3)* in Resources, page 184, for a detailed list of EMF symptoms and clearers.)

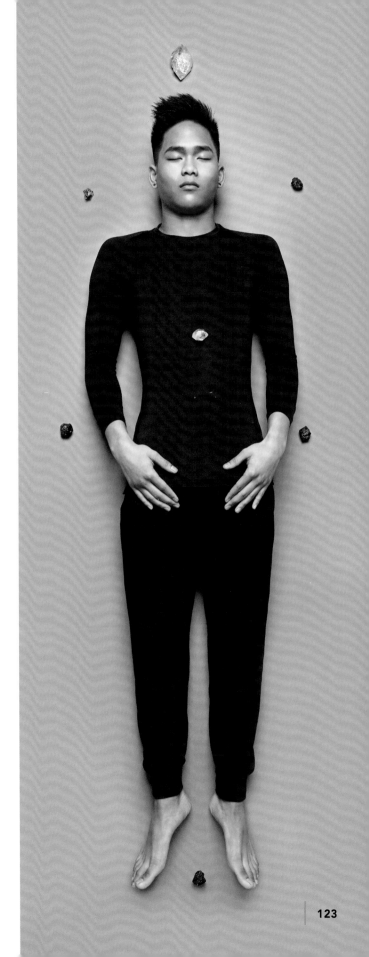

Black Tourmalines form the outer points of a unicursal hexagram around the body with Herkimer Diamond light bringers over the head and on the chest.

Immune stimular crystals in place.

HEART AND IMMUNE SYSTEM

Because crystals harmonize the heart's electrical system with the immune system, the lemniscate grid laid over the heart seed chakra, heart, and higher heart stimulates or soothes the immune system and ensures the heart's well-being. It also balances and aligns the three-chambered heart chakra, connecting you to unconditional, universal love.

Using the grid: This grid can be used at a physical or subtle level of well-being. It is best laid directly onto the body. Place the crystals and then monitor your heartbeat to ascertain whether a different immune-stimulating or immune-soothing crystal needs to be laid over the higher heart (thymus) chakra and the heart seed. If your heart beat speeds up significantly, lay a soothing crystal over the higher heart. If it slows down dramatically, lay an immune stimulator over the higher heart. Lay the crystal with the opposite effect on the heart seed.

Timing: No specific timing required. Use the grid whenever you feel it's necessary.

Color and background: A neutral background works best, because it won't exude vibrations that could interfere with the grid.

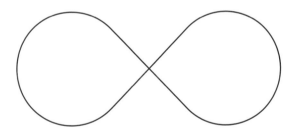

Layout: Lemniscate (see page 54)

YOU WILL NEED:

- 1 grounding crystal for the feet
- 1 pinkish-burgundy crystal or immune stimulator
- 1 emerald-green crystal or immune soother

TO LAY THE GRID:

1. Hold your crystals in your hands and state your intention for the grid.
2. Sit down on the floor.
3. Place a grounding crystal at your feet.
4. Lie down fully.
5. Place one crystal above the heart on the higher heart (thymus) chakra.
6. Place one over the heart seed at the base of the breastbone.
7. Check your heartbeat—it will quickly indicate which crystal should be placed above, and which below. If your heartbeat feels too rapid or is pounding heavily, or if it feels too slow and heavy, switch the crystals around.
8. Use the power of your mind or a crystal wand to trace the lemniscate, crossing the circles over your heart.
9. If dizziness results, breathe deeply and send the energy down toward the crystal at your feet for transmutation.
10. When the layout is complete, remove the crystals in the reverse order in which you laid them. Stand up slowly and ground yourself by stamping your feet.
11. Cleanse the crystals according to the instructions on page 39.

Grid-kit suggestions: Emerald, Emerald Quartz, Fuchsite, Cherry Quartz, Rose Quartz, Ruby, Garnet, Green Aventurine, Lepidolite, Bloodstone, Que Sera, Quantum Quattro, Hematite Quartz, Bloodstone, and grounding crystals (see page 30)

CHAKRA BALANCING

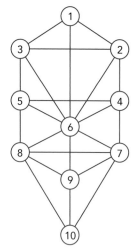

Many Tree of Life layouts end at the base chakra, but this "stretched" layout effectively grounds the energy and centers the whole body, making it much more stable. To bring about an emotional release, you can also lay it so that crystal 6 is on the solar plexus rather than the heart. If you are gridding the crystals on yourself, lie down to check if you have sufficient space, then sit up and start at your feet. (It is much easier if you ask a friend to assist.)

Using the grid: The Tree of Life layout quickly purifies, balances, and re-energizes all the chakras. It is most effective as a chakra balancer when laid over and around the physical body.

Timing: Use the layout whenever you feel out of balance—for instance, if you suffer from a chronic illness or extreme fatigue; if you feel dizzy and disconnected; if you notice you're constantly experiencing minor accidents due to clumsiness; or if you simply feel out of sorts in general.

Color and background: See page 44 for traditional chakra colors. A neutral or graduated color background works best for this layout, however.

YOU WILL NEED:

- 1 grounding crystal
- 1 energizing crystal
- 2 stabilizing crystals
- 1 heart or cleansing crystal, such as Chlorite Quartz
- 2 Blue Lace Agate
- 2 Amethyst
- 1 Clear Quartz or Selenite

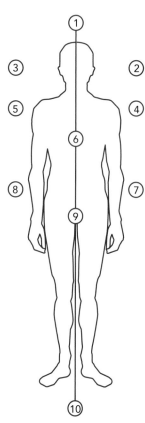

Tree of Life and Tree
of Life on the body

TO LAY THE GRID:

1. Hold the crystals in your hands and state your intention for the grid.
2. Lie down to ensure you have sufficient space.
3. Place a grounding crystal below the feet (position 10), sitting up to do so.
4. Place an energizing crystal over the base chakra (position 9).
5. Place stabilizing crystals on either side of the hips (positions 7 and 8).
6. Place a heart or cleansing crystal over the heart or solar plexus (position 6). Chlorite Quartz or Green Aventurine will work for both.
7. Place Blue Lace Agate on either side of the shoulders (positions 4 and 5).
8. Place Amethyst on either side of the ears (positions 2 and 3).
9. Place Clear Quartz or Selenite over the crown (position 1).
10. Lie still for ten to fifteen minutes, breathing gently.
11. Remove the crystals in the reverse order in which they were laid, then cleanse them according to the instructions on page 39.

Grid-kit suggestions: Grounding crystals (see page 30); chakra crystals (see page 44); Carnelian or Red Jasper; Flint; Chlorite Quartz, Green Aventurine or other cleansing crystal; Rose Quartz; Blue Lace Agate; Amethyst or Auralite 23; Quartz; Petalite; Blue Kyanite or Selenite

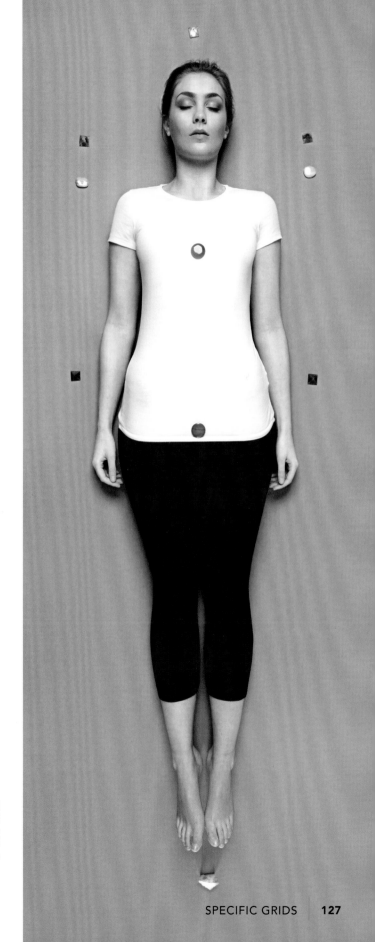

The stretched Tree of Life laid out to balance the chakras and heal the heart.

SUNSHINE SUPER CRYSTALS: THE S.A.D. ANTIDOTE

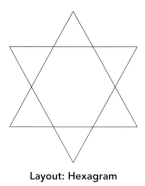

Layout: Hexagram

Many people suffer from "the winter blues," or seasonal affective disorder (S.A.D.), due to a lack of sunlight, but using appropriate sunshine crystals and a layout based on the hexagram can help to counteract that effect. This grid can be laid on and around your body to energetically stimulate the pituitary gland and boost hormone production; or it can be placed in your environment in order to infuse it with solar power. Placing the crystals in the sun for a week or two before the autumnal (fall) equinox charges them up and stores the sunlight in the crystals so that they're ready for the coming winter.

Using the grid: Use the grid for a few minutes daily whenever you find yourself feeling S.A.D., or lay it under your bed. This works especially well during the winter months, but it also helps to boost low moods year-round.

Timing: As a preventative measure, start laying the grid at the autumnal equinox around September 22 and continue until the vernal (spring) equinox on March 20. (Switch the dates around if you live in the southern hemisphere.)

Color and background: Golden or yellow cloth.

YOU WILL NEED:

- 1 clearing crystal such as Shungite, Flint, or Smoky Quartz
- 5 sunshine crystals
- 1 small sunshine keystone

TO LAY THE GRID:

1. Begin by placing the cleansed crystals in the sunshine for one or two weeks prior to the equinox.
2. Hold the crystals in your hands and state your intention for the grid.
3. Place a clearing crystal point-down below your feet or at the base of the layout.
4. Place one sunshine crystal point-down above your head or at the top of the grid.
5. Place a sunshine crystal on either side of your head, level with the bottom of your ears, or on either side of the layout, pointing inward.
6. Hold two sunshine crystals over your groin creases, or place them below the previous two crystals in the layout, pointing inward.
7. Place a small sunshine keystone crystal over your solar plexus or in the center of the layout and restate your intention.
8. Lie quietly for ten to twenty minutes, breathing into your solar plexus and absorbing the crystal energies.

9. When you're ready to stand up, remove the crystals in the reverse order in which they were laid, then cleanse them according to the instructions on page 39. Or, leave the grid under your bed.

10. Place the keystone in your pocket, where you'll feel its energies radiating into your body, and keep it there for as long as you feel connected to it (be sure to cleanse it regularly). When you feel that the crystal has lost its charge, you can repeat the layout after recharging the crystals in sunlight, with a purpose-made essence, or on a large Carnelian first.

11. Place the crystals outside to recharge whenever there is sufficient sunshine.

Grid-kit suggestions: Citrine, Sunstone, Yellow Calcite, Golden Healer Quartz, Celtic Quartz, Quartz, Rutilated Quartz, Tiger's Eye, Orange Kyanite, Carnelian, Golden Azeztulite, Rainbow Mayanite, Mookaite Jasper, Bumble Bee Jasper, Yellow Opal, Yellow Jasper, Zincite

The S.A.D. layout in place over the body. Sunstone crystals beneath the hands.

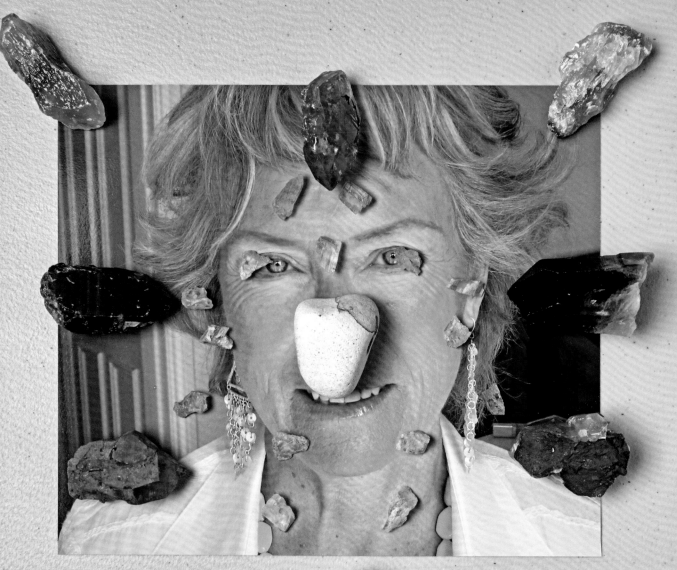

Klinoptilolith is the central keystone in this Smoky Quartz and Gunky Green Ridge hexagram to support during cancer treatment. Green Calcite has been added to soothe nausea and Celtic Golden Healer for overall well-being.

SUPPORT DURING SERIOUS ILLNESS

The Merkaba is an excellent resource if you or someone you know is moving through a serious or chronic illness. It's ideal for emotional and energetic support, and it sends constant healing vibes to the person in need. You might choose a center keystone that's especially suitable for the specific illness, or you might select one that will create centeredness and stability regardless of the condition. Either one works well.

Using the grid: Lay the grid in a place where it will not be disturbed. Under a bed is ideal if it is for your own illness. If not, place it over a photograph of the person.

Timing: Lay the grid as soon as it is needed and leave in place for the duration of the illness. Cleanse it regularly (see page 39).

Color and background: Blue is the traditional color for healing.

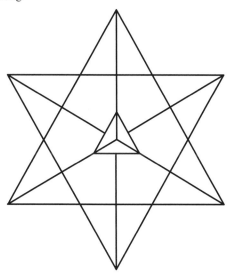

Layout: Merkaba (see page 86)

YOU WILL NEED:

- Appropriate crystals from the grid-kit
- Keystone
- Photograph of the person if they are not present

TO LAY THE GRID:

1. Hold your crystals in your hands and state your intention for the grid.
2. Choose a location where the grid can remain undisturbed.
3. Place the grid over a photograph or the name of the person who needs the support, or place it under your bed or over your own body.
4. Place an appropriate crystal on each of the six outer points.
5. Place a keystone in the center.
6. Join each of the triangles with the power of your mind or a crystal wand.
7. Connect each outer crystal to the central keystone to link the crystals' power.
8. Add additional support crystals if appropriate.
9. Leave the grid in place for as long as necessary. (If you're lying down with the grid on or around your body, lie in place for ten to twenty minutes, or longer if it feels right to you.)
10. When you're ready to dismantle the grid, remove the crystals in the reverse order in which they were laid, and follow the instructions for cleansing on page 39. (For extra cleansing, bury robust crystals such as Smoky Quartz or Flint in the ground after use, and leave delicate crystals in brown rice for an extra day or two.)

Grid-kit suggestions: Eye of the Storm (Judy's Jasper), Shungite, Flint, Jade, Quantum Quattro, Que Sera (Llanoite), Rose Quartz
Cancer support: Klinoptilolith, Smoky Quartz, Rose Quartz, Quartz, Green Ridge Quartz, "Gunky" Golden Healer Quartz, Green Calcite
Neuromuscular conditions: Natrolite and Scolecite, Rhodonite, Red Jasper, Fluorite, Dendritic Agate.

REMOVING A HEADACHE

Headaches and migraines can be debilitating, but a layout of seven crystals pointing inward around your head, with an eighth crystal on your forehead, quickly releases the pressure of a tension headache or a migraine and shuts off the chattering mind, too. This grid is extremely helpful if a restless mind prevents you from sleeping, or if the third eye is stuck in the closed position, causing pressure over it. (In that case, try placing Apophyllite, Rhomboid Selenite, Azurite, or Bytownite over the third eye.)

**Layout: Half a sunburst
(see page 68)**

Using the grid: Lie somewhere quiet where you will be undisturbed for ten to twenty minutes. Place the crystals around your head and let the pressure melt away. Alternatively, place the grid under your pillow.

Timing: Use this grid whenever you need it, but it is particularly potent at a full moon if the headache is due to a blocked third eye.

Color and background: Silver or blue background.

YOU WILL NEED:

- 7 Amethyst or Lapis Lazuli points
- 1 Auralite 23, Amazez or other appropriate crystal
- Anchor stone, if appropriate

TO LAY THE GRID:

1. Hold your crystals in your hands and state your intention for the grid.
2. Place the seven Amethyst points facing inward, so that two will be level with your ears when you lie down; one will be above your head; and the remainder will be evenly spaced in between.
3. Lie down and place the Auralite 23 on your forehead.
4. Place an anchor stone over your heart, if appropriate.
5. Feel the energy of the crystals gathering in the Auralite 23 and radiating through your head, releasing the tension. Lie within the grid for as long as necessary until the pain eases.
6. When the headache has been released, remove the crystals in the reverse order in which they were laid (first the Auralite 23, and then the seven Amethyst points); then cleanse them according to the instructions on page 39.

Grid-kit suggestions: Amethyst, Apophyllite, Chevron Amethyst, Auralite 23, Azurite, Lapis Lazuli, Quartz, Rhomboid Selenite, Bytownite, Labradorite, Azurite

Amethyst is laid around the head, Auralite 23 over the third eye is the keystone, and an anchoring Amethyst crystal is placed over the heart as an anchor stone to soothe emotional turmoil contributing to the headache.

MENTAL CLARITY

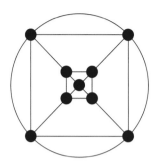

Layout: Expanded square

Mental confusion can arise for a variety of reasons, some of which may require the laying of another grid to heal the underlying causes. But clarity can also be obtained by focusing on a simple, expanded square grid. This is particularly useful when you are preparing to sit for an exam, before a job interview, or whenever you need to express yourself especially clearly. Place an appropriate stone, such as Apophyllite or Fluorite, as the keystone.

Using the grid: Place the grid in your environment or under the head of your bed where it will not be disturbed. Or, lie in the grid, with the top of your head just below the keystone or with the keystone placed on your forehead, if a friend or partner can lay the grid around you.

Timing: No specific timing is necessary. Use this grid whenever the need arises.

Color and background: Yellow is the traditional color for mental clarity.

YOU WILL NEED:

- 4 mental clarity crystals
- 4 anchor crystals
- Crystals for the perimeter, if appropriate
- Keystone

TO LAY THE GRID:

1. Hold your crystals in your hands and state your intention for the grid.
2. Place the four mental clarity crystals on the corners of the inner square. (If you are going to lie in the grid, make the square large enough so that you can comfortably lie down in it.)
3. Place the four anchor crystals on the corners of the outer square.
4. If appropriate, place crystals around the perimeter (dowse to ascertain if required).
5. If you're lying in the grid, lie down now.
6. Place the keystone in the center of the grid, or on your forehead.
7. Use the power of your mind to connect the crystals, moving from the keystone out to the perimeter. Then trace the circle. Move back into the center of the grid and then out again to connect the outer square, then the inner one.
8. If you're laying the grid in your environment, leave it in place as long as you like. As long as you cleanse it regularly, you can leave it in place permanently. Or, if you're lying within the grid, do so for ten to twenty minutes, or longer, if it feels right to you.
9. When you're ready to dismantle the grid, remove the crystals in the reverse order in which they were laid, then cleanse them according to the instructions on page 39.

Grid-kit suggestions: Apophyllite, Fluorite, Auralite 23, Blue Lace Agate, Clear Quartz, Emerald, Dumortierite, Rhomboid Selenite, Azurite, anchor crystals (see page 30).

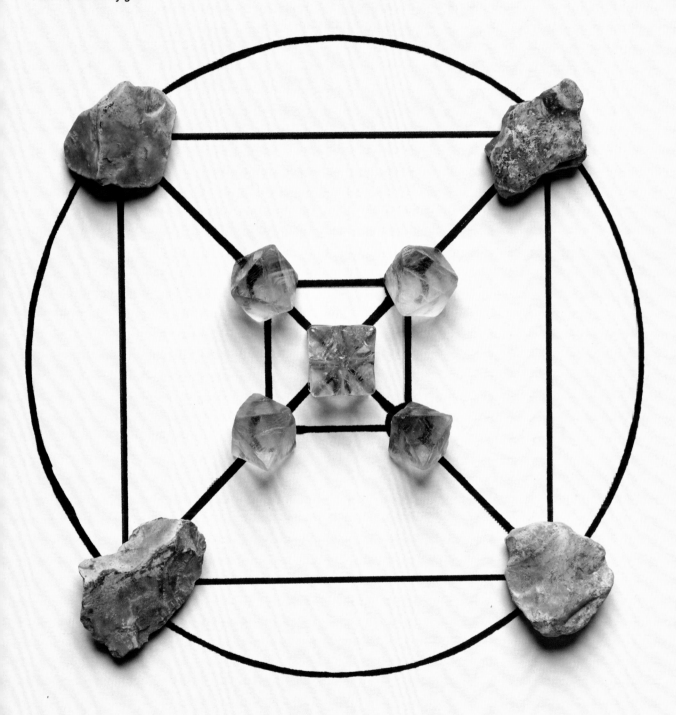

An Amethyst Merkaba forms the central focus of this simple Fluorite and Flint mental clarity grid.

CREATIVITY AND FERTILITY

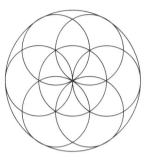

Layout: Seed of Life

The Seed of Life is the central core of the Flower of Life. It is the fundamental point of conception and new beginnings. This grid is perfect for facilitating both physical conception and the inception of a new project.

Using the grid: Lay this grid whenever you are starting a new project, or if you are hoping to conceive a physical or magical child. It can be helpful for inner child work, too.

Timing: Traditionally, a new moon, new year, or spring are the most auspicious times to begin new projects. Avoid the period preceding the winter solstice, as the life force is dormant then—but the period just after the winter solstice is an excellent time for physical conception. Or, lay the grid whenever you conceive a project and tend it carefully.

Color and background: The colors of blood and spring are appropriate backgrounds.

YOU WILL NEED:

- Template
- Keystone
- 6 cleansing crystal points
- 6 manifestation or conception crystals
- 6 activation crystals
- 6 anchor stones

TO LAY THE GRID:

1. Hold your crystals in your hands and state your intention for the grid.
2. Lay the keystone, restating your intention.
3. Lay the six cleansing crystal points on the narrow inner "petals" of the flower, pointing toward the center.
4. Lay the six manifestation or conception crystals at the outer ends of the inner "petals."
5. Lay the six activation crystals on the points of the larger "petals."
6. Use the power of your mind to connect the crystals and to light up the grid. Repeat your intention.
7. Lay the anchoring crystals on the outer perimeter, in line with the cleansing crystals on the inner petals.
8. Leave the grid in place and focus on it daily, keeping your project in mind. Remember to spray-cleanse it if the energy seems to be dissipating. Turn the grid if appropriate after conception occurs.
9. Remove the grid when the project comes to fruition, or replace as appropriate.
10. After you have dismantled the grid by removing the crystals in the reverse order in which they were placed, cleanse them according to the instructions on page 39.

Grid-kit suggestions: Carnelian, Citrine, Chalcedony Tears, Fire Agate, Goldstone, Jade, Orange Kyanite, Menalite, Imperial Topaz, Shiva Lingam, Red Jasper. Cleansing crystals (see page 30), anchoring crystals (see page 30).

The womb-stone Menalite surrounded by six cleansing Smoky Quartz points forms the focus for a conception and creativity grid using Orange Kyanite, Orange Carnelian, and Chalcedony Tears. With the stone facing down, the grid opens the way for conception. Turned the other way, the Menalite holds a space for the project to gestate until it's time for its birth.

ATTRACTING LOVE

We can never have too much love in our lives. This grid either attracts love and romance to you or strengthens a love relationship that already exists. It can be used to radiate love into the world, too. The heart grid is also the perfect forgiveness grid. You might use it to heal an old rift—say, between you and your partner or a friend—or even to send forgiveness to someone who's hurt you in the past. (Dowse, see page 31, or use your intuition to find out which crystals to use, depending on your intention.)

This layout is a great example of how you can create your own grid. I was inspired to make it when I found a heart-shaped mount in an old photo frame in a junkshop, and when I came across some lovely Rose Quartz hearts in a crystal shop. Inspiration can be found anywhere.

Using the grid: Lay the grid to find new love, to strengthen old love, or to send unconditional love to the environment or a specific person.

Timing: The new moon is the traditional time to call in new love, but the grid can be laid at any time to radiate, restore, or strengthen love.

Color and background: Pink, red, or green background. (Pink and red are associated with love and the heart, and green is associated with the heart chakra.)

YOU WILL NEED:

- Sufficient stones to outline the heart shape
- Keystone
- Anchor stone
- High-vibration Twin Flame stone (Twin Flame crystals are two crystals of roughly equal size joined together.)

TO LAY THE GRID:

1. Hold your crystals in your hands and state your intention for the grid.
2. Place crystals around the heart template, breathing mindfully as you do so.
3. If it feels appropriate, place an inner ring of heart stones.
4. Place an anchor stone at the base, or wherever it feels most appropriate.
5. Place the keystone at the center, or wherever it feels most appropriate.
6. Place a high-vibration Twin Flame stone above the grid.
7. Outline the heart with a crystal wand or join it with the power of your heart and mind.
8. Leave the grid in place for as long as it feels necessary to you to attract more love into your life. Remember to cleanse it regularly. Trust your intuition to tell you when to dismantle it.
9. When you're ready to dismantle your grid, remove the crystals in the reverse order in which they were laid, and cleanse them according to the instructions on page 39.

A Mangano Calcite keystone is surrounded by an inner ring of Amethyst and an outer ring of Rose Quartz. Above the grid, a Twin Flame Clear Brandenberg Amethyst radiates spiritual love into the grid. Below the grid, a Twin Flame Smoky Brandenberg Amethyst anchors that love to the earth-plane.

Grid-kit suggestions: Rose Quartz, Rhodochrosite, Rhodonite, Green Aventurine, Larimar, Selenite, Sugilite, Amazonite, Spirit Quartz, Soulmate formation (two crystals attached side by side). Anchor crystals (see page 30). And see *Crystal Love/Love Crystals* in the Resources, page 184.

ABUNDANCE

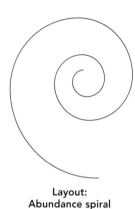

**Layout:
Abundance spiral**

A spiral draws energy into a stagnant situation or clears away negative energy. So if your finances are floundering and you need an infusion of cash, use a spiral grid to clear away anything blocking your abundance—or, if you're seeking a raise or a new job, lay an abundance spiral. Place it over a lottery ticket or a scrap of paper with your wish printed on it. Abundance doesn't just involve money. Abundance is about feeling satisfied and secure with what you have, living an enriching and fulfilling life, sharing life's bounty, showing gratitude, and trusting that the universe will provide appropriately for all your needs.

Using the grid: First, lay the grid with the crystal points pointing up and out to cleanse the energies and remove any blockages to abundance. Cleanse your crystals, then switch, laying the grid with the crystals pointing in toward the center to draw in abundance.

Timing: New moon is the traditional time to begin new projects, but it is also customary to lay an abundance grid under a full moon. If time allows, lay a preparatory clearing grid first, as above, and then lay the second grid. (Remember to cleanse the crystals and the grid space in between.) Leave the grid in place for a moon cycle or until it has completed its work.

Color and background: Green, gold, and yellow are the traditional colors of abundance.

YOU WILL NEED:

- Base for the grid, such as wood, slate, fossilized wood, or golden card or cloth
- Cleansed and empowered Citrine and/or Goldstone
- Cleansed and empowered Herkimer Diamonds or Smoky Quartz
- Cleansed and empowered Goldstone for the keystone
- Anchor stone if appropriate

TO LAY THE GRID:

1. If you're laying a preparatory "cleansing" spiral, start at the topmost point and lay crystals alternately, with the points pointing out from the center. Place the Goldstone in the center as the keystone. If laying an abundance grid, begin by placing the Goldstone in the center, stating that your intention is for it to bring abundance into your life.
2. Lay a spiral of alternated crystals, pointing down and inward, until you reach the Goldstone.
3. Add a grounding stone if appropriate.
4. When the grid is no longer required, dismantle it per the instructions on page 39.

Grid-kit suggestions: Citrine, Goldstone, Green Aventurine, Herkimer Diamond, Jade, Moss Agate, Ruby, Tiger's Eye, Topaz

Abundance crystals are best placed on a base of petrified wood to ground them, but they can be laid as a spiral in the home, preferably on a wooden surface or rock base. This grid is laid on a slate base and utilizes a Flint anchor stone.

CAREER AND LIFEPATH

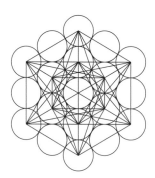

Layout: Metatron's Cube

Although Metatron's Cube looks complex at first glance, it only takes two sets of carefully positioned crystals and a central keystone to clarify complicated situations and take you to the heart of what really matters. Be aware, though, that the answers may present themselves in an unusual, unexpected fashion. For instance, a phrase from a song on the radio might leap out at you and give you the answer—or, a friend may recommend a book to you, or post something relevant and uplifting to you on social media. Metatron's Cube can also be used to help you to gain promotion and advance in your chosen field.

Using the grid: If you are unsure of which path to follow in life, particularly in relation to your career, lay the grid and ask for guidance. Affirm that the perfect opportunity manifests with perfect timing. If you are seeking promotion, lay the grid before approaching your boss with the request, or before interviewing for a new position.

Timing: Ideally, you should lay the Cube at a new moon and expect an answer by the full moon. Afterward, the grid can be dismantled.

Color and background: Gold, silver, or a color that is compatible with your intended career. For example, if you were in medicine, you might choose blue, the traditional color of healing; or, if you were in banking, you might choose yellow or gold to represent "abundance" or money. A natural base of stone or wood is practical and pragmatic, too, grounding the answer in the everyday.

A tumbled Pietersite for insight is surrounded by tumbled Citrine, Smoky Herkimer Diamonds, and Carnelian points. The grid is anchored with Flint.

YOU WILL NEED:

- Template
- 6 career and/or lifepath crystals (see grid-kit suggestions below)
- 6 grounding crystals
- Keystone
- Crystal wand

TO LAY THE GRID:

1. Hold your crystals in your hands and state your intention for the grid.
2. Lay six career or lifepath crystals around the central hexagon.
3. Lay six grounding stones around the outer hexagon.
4. Add additional clearing stones around the perimeter if appropriate.
5. Lay the keystone in the center to fire up the grid.
6. Move a crystal wand from each of the outer crystals into the center. (Use a crystal wand for this grid, as it is complex and best joined with a wand to clarify the energy flow.) Restate your intention.
7. Breathe steadily for a few moments, focusing your eyes on the grid. Then gently disconnect from it, and leave it undisturbed in your environment, letting it do its work. Leave the grid in place until you receive your answer.
8. When you're ready to dismantle your grid, remove the crystals in the reverse order in which they were laid, then cleanse them according to the instructions on page 39.

Grid-kit suggestions: Blue Jade, Carnelian, Citrine, Green Aventurine, Green Tourmaline, Moss Agate, Rose Quartz, Turquoise, Tiger's Eye, Septarian. Grounding crystals (see page 30)

Lifepath crystals: Eudialyte, Turquoise, Strawberry Lemurian Seed, Pietersite, "Life Path" crystal (which is long, thin, and clear, with one or more absolutely smooth sides)

CRYSTAL GLOSSARY

CARNELIAN

Carnelian stimulates courage and action. It restores motivation, energizes the soul body, and helps turn dreams into realities. With this stone, you can work an act of truly outrageous magic that transmogrifies the mundane world. For instance, use it to successfully apply for a dream job, for which you are not qualified, where you dramatically transform other people's lives.

FLINT

Flint assists detoxification and pain release. Its power heals at emotional, psychological, and energetic levels rather than physical. Metaphorically, it cuts through blockages, past-life ties, and chakra connections that you have outgrown. Taking you deep into yourself, Flint reveals and transmutes underlying causes of depression. It assists you in bringing your shadow's gifts into conscious awareness. It creates core stability and restructures information stored in the cells. By cutting away all that no longer serves you, it sets you free from the past.

PIETERSITE

Pietersite promotes "walking your truth." It can be used for a vision quest or shamanic journey and it accesses a high state of altered awareness. It removes conditioning imposed by other people and links you to your inner guidance.

GREEN AVENTURINE

Green Aventurine protects the spleen chakra from energy vampires and also protects against EMF emissions. It is a great stone to accompany you outside your comfort zone, as it provides courage and encouragement.

INNER-SELF MEDITATION

Layout: Labyrinth

Drawing a Labyrinth is a meditation in itself, but placing the crystals and slowly walking the Labyrinth on the ground (or with your finger or a crystal point) really shifts your brainwaves into a more relaxed meditative state that combines alpha, the initial relaxation state, with the brainwaves of expanded consciousness. It takes you into the theta state, which is associated with visualization and effortless problem-solving. Resting for a while at the center of the crystal Labyrinth moves you into delta, an even deeper state of awareness in which you remain highly alert yet totally relaxed, since alpha waves are still at work. Delta brainwaves are long and slow, like the resonant beat of a drum deep within you.

This type of deep relaxation and intense focus creates an alert state of awareness that is nevertheless deeply meditative. Within this state, anything can be manifested. With practice, it only takes a few minutes to shift into this combined brainwave pattern.

Using the grid: Use this grid as a focus for contemplation, relaxation, and meditation, or for problem-solving.

Timing: This grid is particularly potent laid at the dark, new, and full moons, but walking the Labyrinth can also be a weekly or even a daily meditation.

Color and background: Labyrinths are traditionally laid on the ground, drawn on stone, or carved from wood. Place your Labyrinth on a background color that complements your intention.

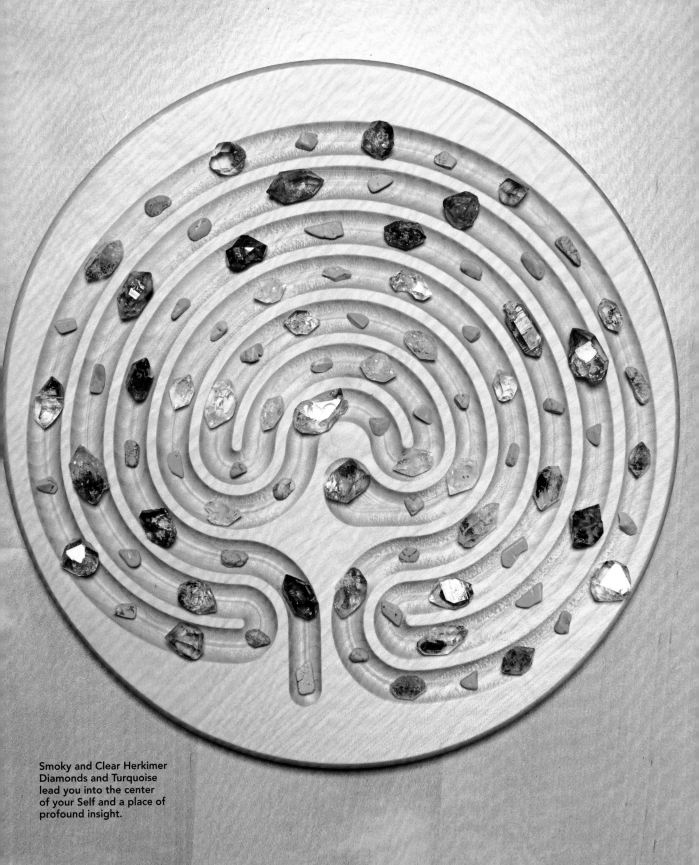

Smoky and Clear Herkimer
Diamonds and Turquoise
lead you into the center
of your Self and a place of
profound insight.

YOU WILL NEED:

- Labyrinth board or template
- Sufficient crystals to outline the Labyrinth
- Keystone

TO LAY THE GRID:

1. Mark out your template or place your board in front of you.
2. Hold your crystals in your hands (or place your hands over them if you're laying a large outdoor grid).
3. Place each crystal slowly, using focused concentration.
4. When the Labyrinth outline is complete, slowly walk into the center with your feet, finger, or crystal wand.
5. Pause at the center for several minutes. Focus on your breath, and sense a deep connection with your inner Self and with everything around you. (Avoid focusing on a specific intention or outcome. The idea is to achieve "no-mind," an intensely meditative state.)
6. Walk out again, leaving the crystals in place ready for the next journey inward.
7. Leave the grid in place for as long as necessary, trusting your intuition to tell you when to dismantle it. This is a complicated grid, so you won't want to lay it over again each time you use it.
8. To dismantle the grid, remove the crystals in the reverse order in which you laid them, then cleanse them according to the instructions on page 39.

Grid-kit suggestions: Ammolite, Ammonite, high-vibration and meditative crystals, Anandalite™, Petalite, Azeztulite, Elestial Smoky Quartz, Elestial Rose Quartz, Selenite, Lemurian Seed, Celtic Healer, Tibetan Quartz, Herkimer Diamond, Amazez, Turquoise; robust outdoor crystals such as Quartz, Rose Quartz, raw Labradorite, or Smoky Quartz

CRYSTAL GLOSSARY

CLEAR HERKIMER DIAMOND

Herkimers transform the way you see the world. They aid you in creating within the physical body new neural pathways that connect to the lightbody and to All That Is to manifest your spiritual potential on earth. Herkimer attunes you to a much higher reality and accelerates your spiritual growth, so you become coherent at every level of being.

LABRADORITE

Labradorite provides a protective shield between you and the outside world. Stimulating metaphysical gifts, it reaches into multidimensions to contact the spiritual world.

LEMURIAN SEED

An extremely effective connector and activator for grids, Lemurian Seed crystal has an exceptionally high vibration that assists in the evolution of the planet. It contains knowledge from ancient Lemuria and beyond.

CELESTITE

One of the major angel connectors, Celestite stimulates clairvoyance and promotes dream recall and out-of-body journeys. It teaches you how to trust in the infinite wisdom of the universe. A crystal for conflict resolution, it instills balance in times of stress.

ANGELIC COMMUNICATION

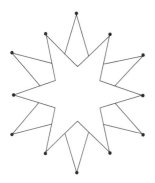

Layout: Twelve-pointed star

The twelve-pointed star is a symbol traditionally associated with the angelic realm, and it can be used to make contact with your guardian angel or the archangel of your choice. You might wish to contact an angel if you need to feel protected, or to feel as if someone were holding your hand and guiding you through a particularly difficult time in your life. Or, you may wish to send this kind of loving protection to watch over another person—such as a child, for instance. This grid is particularly suited to placing on a home altar. (This does not indicate that you are worshipping the archangel in question; rather, that you simply wish to connect to the angelic realm.)

Using the grid: Place a keystone in the center of the grid according to the angel or archangel with whom you wish to make contact.

Timing: Lay the grid at any time. You can also use it for daily meditation.

Color and background: You may wish to lay your grid on a color associated with a specific archangel (see the list on page 153) or to use a background in a non-specific color such as light blue, silver, or gold.

This angelic star layout uses Lapis Lazuli and Herkimer Diamonds to connect to arch-angel Michael, an important grid-keeper and protector.

YOU WILL NEED:

- 12 angelic crystals
- Archangel keystone

TO LAY THE GRID:

1. Hold your crystals in your hands and state your intention for the grid.
2. Lay a crystal on each point of the star, working in a clockwise direction.
3. Place your keystone in the center and call on your chosen archangel to be present, or invite your guardian angel to move closer to you. Keep an open mind, and ask your angel to indicate its presence to you. You may hear the beat of angelic wings or celestial music; you might feel a cool breeze running over you; or you may simply notice a deep sense of comfort and unconditional love surrounding you.
4. Leave the grid in place for as long as you feel you need to—perhaps fifteen to twenty minutes, or place it permanently on your altar.
5. When you're ready to dismantle your grid, remove the crystals in the reverse order in which they were laid, then cleanse them according to the instructions on page 39.

Grid-kit suggestions: Archangel crystals in accordance with the colors listed opposite; Angel's Wing Calcite, Angelite, Blue Celestite, Amphibole Quartz, Anandalite™ (Aurora Quartz), Angel Aura Quartz, Larimar, Lilac Selenite, Seraphinite, Rutilated Quartz, Vera Cruz Amethyst

Archangel Colors and Qualities

ARCHANGEL	COLOR	QUALITY
Ariel	pale pink	confidence, manifestation
Atrugiel	red, black/smoky	protection
Azrael	creamy white	comfort, transition
Chamuel	pale green	peace, finder of lost things
Gabriel	copper, white	revelation
Haniel	pale blue, translucent	harmony, intuition
Jeremiel	dark purple	prophecy, inspiration
Jophiel	dark pink, magenta	wisdom, beauty
Lucifer	pure white, clear	transformation
Melchizedek	silver/gold	bringing in light
Metatron	violet, pink, green	expansion
Michael	lilac, royal purple, royal blue, gold	courage, esoteric understanding
Raguel	pale blue, blue-green	harmonious relationship
Raphael	emerald green	healing
Raziel	rainbow colors	spiritual insight, Akashic keeper
Sandalphon	turquoise	truth
Uriel	yellow, red	ideas
Zadkiel	purple, deep indigo blue	compassion, forgiveness

SPIRITUAL EXPANSION: MEETING A DRAGON MENTOR

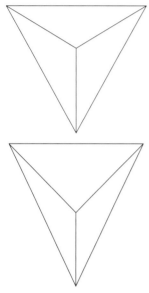

Layout: Dragon's Eye

The Dragon's Eye is a powerful attractor for a spirit mentor or power animal ally, particularly a dragon, or an earth or star being. (An earth being could be a deva—a nature spirit—or an earth spirit or a dragon, while a star being comes from outside this universe and has your highest good in mind.) As powerful archetypal energies, the dragons are moving ever closer into human awareness, for they have expressed the desire to assist with the spiritual evolution of the Earth. They are allied to the four cardinal directions and to both "above" and "below," or heaven and earth. They also connect to the elements of fire, earth, air, water, metal, and spirit, as you'll see in the box on page 156. To attract a dragon mentor, place a suitable crystal dragon carving in the center of the Eye.

Using the grid: Lay the grid to call in a power animal ally, dragon, or earth or star being mentor to help you overcome challenges on your journey through life.

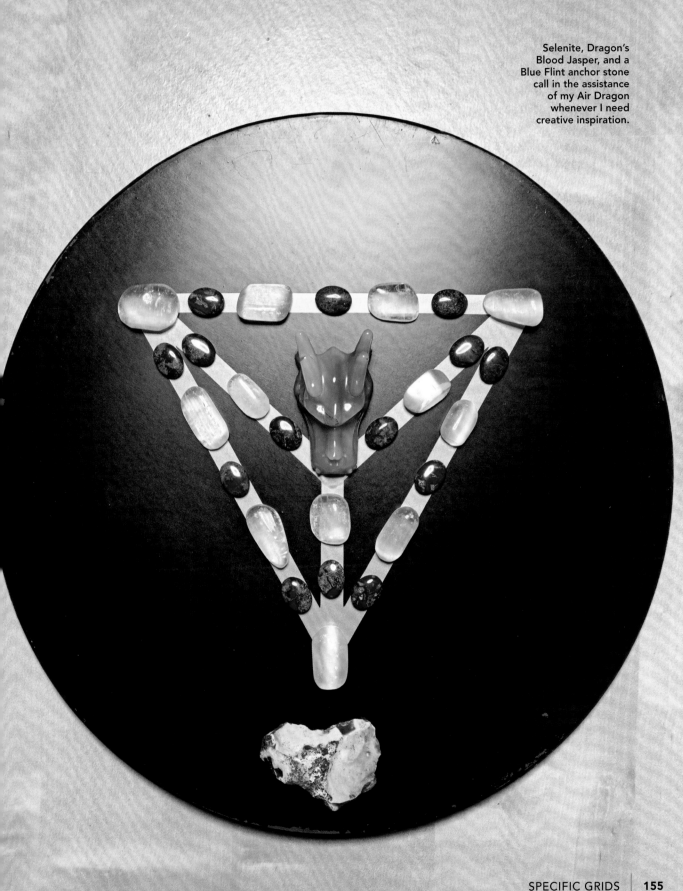

Selenite, Dragon's Blood Jasper, and a Blue Flint anchor stone call in the assistance of my Air Dragon whenever I need creative inspiration.

YOU WILL NEED:

- Earth, fire, water crystals and/or Dragon's Blood Jasper crystals
- Selenite (or appropriate elemental crystals) to outline the grid
- Dragon carving or appropriate crystal to act as the keystone

TO LAY THE GRID:

1. Choose an area where you can leave the grid in place undisturbed for an extended period of time.
2. Hold your crystals in your hands and state your intention. (You might call on a specific dragon as you do so, but you can also simply remain open to intuitively attracting exactly the right dragon or being for your purpose, in which case, choose a mixture of elemental crystals and alternate them in the layout.)
3. Lay an elemental stone at the base of the Y.
4. Lay an elemental stone on either side of the V.
5. Surround the Y with elemental crystals and/or intersperse with anchoring Dragon's Blood Jasper.
6. Place an appropriate keystone or dragon carving in the center.

Elemental Colors and Crystals

ELEMENT	COLOR	CRYSTALS
Earth	Green	Flint, Kambaba Jasper, Rainforest Jasper, Smoky Quartz, Eye of the Storm (Judy's Jasper), Stromatolite, Kiwi Jasper, Plumite, Agate, Moss Agate, Green Kyanite, Picrolite, Bloodstone, Dragon's Blood Jasper
Air	Yellow	Yellow Calcite, Golden Healer Quartz, Apophyllite, Yellow Aventurine, Amethyst, Angel or Opal Aura Quartz, Agate, Herkimer Diamond, Yellow Kyanite (Hiddenite), Selenite
Fire	Red/Orange	Fire Agate, Poppy Jasper, Red Zincite, Carnelian, Firework Obsidian, Sunstone, Orange Kyanite, Celtic Golden Healer, Red Jasper
Water	Blue	Indicolite Quartz, Blue Tourmaline, Blue Calcite, Blue Celtic Healer, Blue Kyanite, Chrysocolla, Turquoise
Metal	Silver	Iron Pyrite, Native Copper, Mohawkite, Stibnite, Galena, Healer's Gold
"Ether"	Transparent/Gold	Libyan Gold Tektite, Moldavite, Quartz, Trigonic Quartz, Anandalite, Selenite

7. Ask the dragon to make itself known to you. If you have placed a crystal dragon in the center of your grid, pick up the dragon and hold it in your hands so that it becomes a home for your dragon-being. You'll know when the dragon is present. You might feel very hot or cold; you might feel a breeze blowing or experience powerful shivers. Or you might actually sense or "see" the dragon with your third eye.

8. Whenever you need guidance, hold the dragon in your hands. (Once you've attracted a dragon, it stays connected to the statue permanently. There's no need to cleanse the statue in the usual way.)

9. Leave the grid in place long term. When you want to banish the dragon from your space, thank the dragon for its assistance and simply remove the crystals. Dragons are highly intelligent beings who instinctively know when their presence and assistance is required, and when it isn't.

Dragon mentors and their characteristics

• The creative fire dragon of the East symbolizes energy, transmutation, and mastery of power. A fire dragon lends you the courage to overcome obstacles.

• The nurturing earth dragon of the West connects you to your inner riches, your resources, and your potential. Earth dragons facilitate grounding and stabilizing. Dragons of integration, they pull together scattered energies.

• The inspirational air dragon of the North facilitates insight and illumination. This dragon offers clarity and connection to your inner guidance or intuition.

• The empathetic water dragon of the South connects you to your deepest feelings and to the hidden desires that motivate you. Call on one to link you to significant ancestral memories. The water dragon helps you to come to terms with, and release, the past.

• The assertive metal dragons regulate the passage of the lifeforce within the Earth's meridians and can be called on to assist with earth-healing—both for your immediate environment and for the planet as a whole. Their steely resolve is helpful if you need to stand up for yourself or take on a challenge.

• The great cosmic dragons are vast interstellar beings, wise beyond the range of human perception. Mythical and mystical, they guide human and planetary evolution and carry the wisdom of the ages.

PAST LIFE

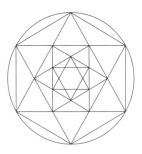

**Layout:
Infinite Hexagram**

Although you might not be aware of it, your past lives may well be influencing your present one. This layout is intended to access the Akashic record—the record of all that has been, could be, and ever will be—to clear blockages arising from past life experiences (in whatever timeframe those experiences may have occurred). While this grid does not give details of past lives, you may find that it offers glimpses into them as you continue to work with it.

Using the grid: Lay this grid if you feel blocked or stuck, or if you identify a negative pattern in your life. If, as you lay or contemplate the grid, you discover something that needs healing or reframing, place an appropriate crystal in the relevant portion of the Infinite Hexagram or Sri Yantra variation (as shown in the grid photographed) and leave it in place until no longer necessary. For instance, if you become aware of a childhood trauma, you might choose a Pink Agate crystal and place it in an inner portion of the grid. Use your intuition or dowse (see page 31) to decide which portion of the grid should hold the crystal representing this issue.

Timing: This grid is particularly potent when laid during the dark of the moon.

Color and background: Indigo and purples.

This Sri Yantra past life healing grid was laid around a Variscite keystone. Smoky Quartz cleansed the grid and Herkimer Diamonds re-energized it. Turquoise was used for past life healing and Brandenberg Amethysts returned the soul to a state of perfect purity. A Flint anchored the grid into present day reality.

YOU WILL NEED:

- A crystal for each major crossing point, depending on the size of the grid (dowse, see page 31, to decide which crystals and positions to use)
- Light-bringing crystals, for the lines connecting the outer hexagram if using the Infinite Hexagram
- Grounding and clearing crystals for the perimeter
- Crystals for issues that might surface as you lay the grid (dowse, see page 31, or intuit to identify which crystals are appropriate)
- Keystone

Note: The grid photographed utilizes a Sri Yantra pre-cut form that held the crystals securely within it.

TO LAY THE GRID:

1. Hold your crystals in your hands and state your intention for the grid.
2. Place crystals on the three points of the downward-facing triangle in the center of the grid.
3. Place crystals on the three points of the upward-facing triangle in the center of the grid.
4. Moving outward, place crystals on the two triangles forming the next hexagram.
5. Moving outward again, place crystals on the two triangles forming the outer hexagram. (You can expand this by adding further hexagrams if you wish. Simply draw them on the template or outline them with crystals.)
6. Place light-bringing crystals midway along the lines connecting the outer hexagrams.
7. Place grounding and clearing crystals around the perimeter.
8. Place the keystone in the center, restating your intention.
9. Quietly contemplate the grid with softly focused eyes. If an issue or memory arises, place a crystal in the appropriate part of the grid. Continue this contemplation for as long as it feels right to you.
10. Cleanse the grid (see page 39).
11. Return to the grid when appropriate. (As you work with long-term grids such as this one—or like the S.A.D. grid on page 128—you'll soon be able to recognize when an issue needs revisiting, and when a grid needs a recharge.)
12. When the grid has completed its work, dismantle it from the inside, thanking the crystals for their work.
13. Cleanse the crystals and clear the grid space with sound or clearing spray (see page 39); otherwise, the geometric effect of this grid has a tendency to linger.

Grid-kit suggestions: Apophyllite, Azeztulite, Brandenberg Amethyst, Celtic Quartz, Chrysotile (use in tumbled form, wash hands after use), Dumortierite, Lepidolite, Kambaba Jasper, Merlinite, Moldavite, Phenacite, Petrified Wood, Phantom Quartz, Preseli Bluestone, Record Keeper, Stromatolite, Trigonic Quartz, Lemurian Seed, Cradle of Life (Humankind), Tanzanite, Tibetan Quartz. (See *Crystal Prescriptions (volume 6)* in the Resource, page 184 for crystals to heal past-life issues.)

CRYSTAL GLOSSARY

BRANDENBERG AMETHYST

The Brandenberg Amethyst brings about deep soul healing and forgiveness. It is the finest tool available for removing implants, attachments, spirit possession, or mental influence, and this is the stone par excellence for transformation or transition.

VARISCITE

Helpful for past life exploration, Variscite facilitates visual images while going deeply into the feelings of appropriate lives, stimulating insight and helping one reframe situations. This stone facilitates moving out of deep despair and into a position of trust with Universe.

TANZANITE

High-vibration Tanzanite facilitates altered states of consciousness and stimulates metaphysical abilities, linking to archangels and Ascended Masters. Accelerating spiritual growth, it downloads information from the Akashic record to dissolve outdated karmic dis-ease.

PRESELI BLUESTONE

Powerfully magnetic, Preseli Bluestone provides an inner compass to show you the way. It grounds healing energy into the planet or the body and is a powerful antidote to EMF emissions.

TRANQUILITY

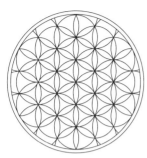

Layout: Flower of Life

The Flower of Life is essentially a grid of tranquility. It radiates peace and goodwill into the environment, and you can lay on it any intuitive pattern that feels right to you. It is best laid on the template, so that the underlying geometry connects the crystals. That way, you don't need to place one on every single point. Lay the Flower of Life if you think you may be coming to the end of a tumultuous period in your life and want to invite calm and tranquility into your daily experience, or if you're surrounded by upheaval and stress in your home or workplace—due, perhaps, to rebellious teenage children, or to pressure from your boss.

Using the grid: Choose a place where the grid will not be disturbed and leave it to do its work. (For more on using the Flower of Life, see the advanced grid on page 76.)

Timing: No specific timing is necessary. Lay the grid at any time.

Color and background: The Flower of Life can be laid on any color or background material, but using wood or other natural materials helps the peaceful energy to anchor itself. Beautiful, purpose-made boards are readily available.

YOU WILL NEED:

- Template
- Sufficient crystals to lay the pattern you choose on the grid (dowse, see page 31, or use your intuition to select your crystals.)
- At least 1 anchor stone (but 4 to 6 are ideal)
- Keystone for the center

TO LAY THE GRID:

1. Hold the crystals in your hands and state your intention for the grid.
2. Begin by laying the keystone in the center and restating your intention.
3. Create a pattern around the Flower of Life, placing at least one anchor stone on the outer ring, but preferably four to six. (You can create any pattern you like within the grid. For example, you could create only a single central flower, if that feels right to you, or you could fill in the whole outer ring of petals.)
4. Place light-bringing crystals (see page 30) around the perimeter.
5. Leave the grid in place to do its work for as long as necessary—permanently, if required.
6. To dismantle this grid, simply remove the crystals—the energy will dissipate on its own after the crystals are removed, so no cleansing is required.

Grid-kit suggestions: Rose Quartz, Selenite, Rhodochrosite, Quartz, Labradorite, Kyanite, Eye of the Storm (Judy's Jasper), Smoky Quartz

This sphere of tranquility centers around
Rose Quartz and Rhodochrosite, outlined by
Black Tourmaline and Herkimer Diamonds.
The green circle is Kyanite interspersed
with Amethyst, surrounded by further Rose
Quartz and Selenite. The outer circle
is Amethyst, and Smoky Quartz
anchor the cardinal points.

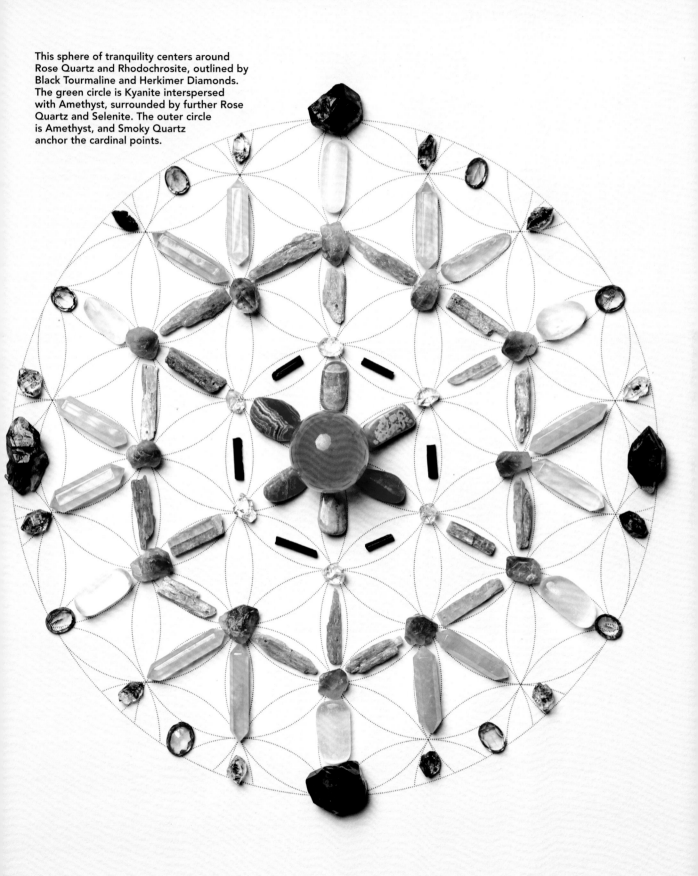

JOY AND REJUVENATION

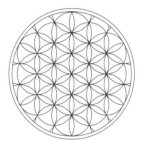

Layout: Flower of Life

Lay the Joy and Rejuvenation grid to revitalize your daily experience or to bring about social change and regeneration. This joyful grid demonstrates just how color can affect and interact with a grid. Use bright pink stones instead of the green in the Tranquility Grid, and the Flower of Life radiates joy and rejuvenation into an area that has become energetically dead. That may be into a part of your own life or that of a community, into over-cultivated soil, or even into a whole country. It is helpful for a community that has grown apathetic following a loss, shock, or trauma and which needs to regenerate itself. The grid enthusiastically activates the energies and gets things moving. It is particularly helpful where depression and hopelessness have taken over, or if you're surrounded by apathy in the workplace or in community matters, as it also strengthens motivation and a desire to get things done. You don't have to be personally involved to lend energetic support in this way. Color-coated crystals were chosen to infuse vitality, as this vibrant color is difficult to source as points in a natural form. As with the Sphere of Tranquility on page 162, this joyful grid is best laid on a template so that the underlying geometry connects the crystals and radiates the energies outward.

Form: On the Flower of Life background, lay any shape that intuitively feels right to you.

Using the grid: Choose a place where the grid will not be disturbed and leave it to do its work. (For more on using the Flower of Life, see the advanced grid on page 76.)

Timing: No specific timing is necessary. Lay the grid at any time.

Color and background: Anchoring and radiating material such as wood, slate, or the earth helps the rejuvenating energy to ground itself in the everyday world. Bright-colored backgrounds assist in spreading the joy. Beautiful, purpose-made boards are readily available.

This joy and rejuvenation grid centers around a Selenite ball and coated Rose Aura Quartz outlined by Black Tourmaline and Herkimer Diamonds. Rose Aura "petals" lead to a Rose Aura circle interspersed with natural Rhodolite Garnets. The next petal circle combines Rose Quartz and Selenite. The outer circle is Amethyst, Smoky Herkimers, and double terminated Smoky Quartz to anchor the cardinal points, with further Rose Aura points to direct the energy out into the community.

YOU WILL NEED:

- Template
- Sufficient crystals to lay the pattern (dowse, see page 31, to select your crystals or use your intuition.)
- At least 1 anchor stone (4 to 6 are ideal)
- Keystone for the center

TO LAY THE GRID:

1. Hold the crystals in your hands and state your intention for the grid.
2. Begin by laying the keystone in the center and restating your intention.
3. Create a pattern around the keystone, placing at least one anchor stone on the outer ring, but preferably four to six.
4. Place appropriate crystals (see grid-kit suggestions below) around the perimeter.
5. Leave the grid in place to do its work for as long as necessary—permanently, if required.
6. To dismantle this grid, simply remove the crystals—the energy will slowly dissipate on its own after the crystals are removed, so no cleansing is required.

Grid-kit suggestions: Rose or Ruby Aura Quartz, Cobalto Calcite, Rhodolite Garnet, Erythrite, Rose Quartz, Selenite, Quartz, Herkimer Diamond, Red Kyanite, Poppy Jasper, Hematite Quartz
Anchoring: Eye of the Storm (Judy's Jasper), Polychrome Jasper, Smoky Quartz, Hematite, Red Flint

CRYSTAL GLOSSARY

SELENITE

Selenite accesses angelic consciousness and brings divine light into everything it touches. A powerful transmutor for emotional energy, Selenite releases core feelings behind psychosomatic illnesses and emotional blockages.

ROSE AURA QUARTZ

Rose Aura Quartz works to transmute deeply held doubts about self-worth, bestowing the gift of unconditional love of yourself and making a powerful connection to universal love.

SUGILITE

A natural tranquilizer, gentle Sugilite is particularly helpful for children—or anyone—who feel like misfits. It prevents bullying and assists with reading capacity.

RHODOCHROSITE

One of the major healing "love stones," Rhodochrosite encourages the expression of feelings and encourages forgiveness of the past. This compassionate stone draws love to you and comforts those who are alone.

CHILDREN

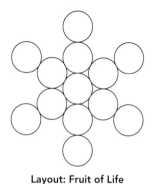

Layout: Fruit of Life

The Fruit of Life, which is contained within the Flower of Life, helps to support children and bring out their highest potential by creating a stable environment for them. This grid can be tailored to an individual child's needs. The central ring of crystals can be changed to help them meet the challenges they face, so this grid can be left in place long term. (See the grid-kit suggestions below for assistance with issues your child may be facing.) Children enjoy being with crystals, so actively involve them in choosing and laying the grid crystals—always under your supervision, of course—and place grids out of the reach of small children.

Using the grid: The grid can be laid in an older child's or teenager's room, but a grid for young children should always be placed high up out of reach.

Timing: The grid can be laid at any time, but it is particularly useful when a child is facing any kind of challenge or exhibiting challenging behavior.

Color and background: Choose a color that is supportive and calming for the child's challenge or issue. For instance, if your child struggles with reading and writing, lay a dyslexia grid on pale creamy yellow (research shows that brown text on cream paper is easier for a dyslexic child to read). If your child is being bullied, a soft pink base softens the aggression, while a pale orange one supports the courage the child needs to overcome this.

YOU WILL NEED:

- Central keystone to represent your child
- 6 "issue" or calming stones
- 4 grounding crystals
- 2 light-bringing crystals

TO LAY THE GRID:

1. Hold your crystals in your hands and state your intention for the grid.
2. Lay the central keystone to represent your child.
3. Lay six crystals around the keystone to assist with the challenge or issue. (These crystals can either represent a single issue, or different ones—whichever feels best to you. However, it may be more effective to address separate issues by laying individual grids.)
4. Lay four grounding crystals to anchor the grid at each corner of the "square."
5. Lay a light-bringing crystal at the top and bottom.
6. Leave in place until the issue or issues have been resolved, remembering to cleanse the grid regularly.

Grid-kit suggestions: Crackle Quartz, Pink Agate, Coprolite ("Dinosaur Poo"), Fuchsite, Howlite, Rose Quartz, Turquenite, Youngite
Examinations and concentration: Orange Kyanite, Fluorite, Rose Quartz, Green Aventurine
Communication: Blue Lace Agate, Pink Agate, Blue Crackle Quartz, Youngite, Chinese Writing Stone, Chrysanthemum Stone, Sodalite

This Fruit of Life grid was laid out without a background template by a child who was struggling to learn to read. The anchor stone is Sugilite, which also surrounds the central Quartz heart that the child chose to represent himself, together with Amethyst for mental clarity. Smoky Quartz and Selenite acted as anchors and light-bringers.

Autism: Muscovite, Sugilite, Charoite, Moldavite, Fuchsite, Sodalite, Lapis Lazuli, Amethyst, Lepidolite, Turquoise
ADHD: Lepidolite, Lithium Quartz, Kunzite, Rutilated Quartz
Dyslexia: Sugilite, Blue Crackle Quartz, Sodalite, Fuchsite, Emerald Quartz, Amethyst
Dyspraxia: Black Moonstone, Sugilite, Lepidolite, Muscovite, Cherry Quartz

Temper tantrums: Rose Quartz, Blue Lace Agate, Howlite, Pink Crackle Quartz, Rose Aura Quartz
Nightmares: Chrysoprase, Amethyst, Prehnite, Bloodstone.

HARMONIOUS RELATIONSHIPS

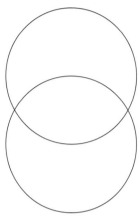

Layout: Vesica Piscis

The Vesica Piscis brings people together in harmonious relationships—and that's not limited only to marriages or other romantic partnerships. This grid is also advantageous for work colleagues, friends, business associates, and anyone else in your life with whom you've had a misunderstanding or need to harmonize ideas.

Using the grid: Lay the grid whenever you want to bring two people together for mutual benefit or to soothe disagreements.

Timing: No specific timing is required. Lay the grid whenever it is necessary.

Color and background: A pink background works well for the Vesica Piscis. If a relationship needs grounding in the everyday rather than the fantasy world, lay it on a natural material, such as stone or wood.

YOU WILL NEED:

- Sufficient crystals to outline the two circles
- Shiva Lingam or other appropriate keystone

TO LAY THE GRID:

1. Hold your crystals in your hands and state your intention for the grid.
2. Outline the left-hand circle in crystals first.
3. Outline the right-hand (overlapping) circle next.
4. Place the keystone in the center and restate your intention.
5. Leave in place for as long as you feel is necessary to keep the relationship on track, cleansing the grid regularly.
6. To dismantle the grid, remove the crystals in the order in which they were laid, then cleanse them according to the instructions on page 39.

Grid-kit suggestions: Rose Quartz, Selenite, Smoky Quartz, Rhodochrosite, Rhodonite, Green Aventurine, Agate, Watermelon Tourmaline, Pink and Green Tourmalines, Turquoise, Shiva Lingam, Twin Flame (two crystals springing side by side from the same base)

Rose Quartz and Rhodonite circles around a Green Aventurine Merkaba keystone restore unconditional love to a mature partnership.

EMF AND TOXIC EARTH ENERGY CLEARING

Layout: Square

A basic square grid can be expanded into a powerful layout that clears and protects a space, transmuting geoelectromagnetic fields and toxic earth energies. Try laying your grid with Shungite. It contains "bucky balls," hexagonal molecular structures that absorb negative emanations, and it may be the most effective EMF solution there is.

Using the grid: Lay this grid wherever a space is invaded by EMFs or is crisscrossed by toxic earth energy lines (dowse, see page 31, to check whether this is so, and if so, where they are placed). The grid can either be laid around a room or placed within it to expand to energetically fill the space.

Timing: No specific timing is required. Lay the grid whenever it is needed.

Color and background: This grid is best laid on a natural background, such as wood or slate.

YOU WILL NEED:

- 4 clearing and transmutation crystals
- 4 anchoring crystals
- Keystone

TO LAY THE GRID:

1. Hold your crystals in your hands and state your intention for the grid.
2. Place four clearing and transmutation crystals on the inside corners of the square.
3. Place four anchoring crystals on the outside corners of the square.
4. Place the keystone in the center and restate your intention.
5. Join up the corners of the square with a crystal wand or the power of your mind.
6. Leave the grid in place for as long as necessary, even permanently, cleansing frequently.

Grid-kit suggestions: Shungite, Black Tourmaline, Herkimer Diamond, Amethyst, Green Aventurine. Anchoring stones (see page 30).

A Flint keystone on slate is surrounded by four Golden
Herkimer Diamonds and anchored by four polished
Shungite discs to protect against EMF disturbances.

PERSON TO PERSON

Layout: Sunburst

Grids can be used to send distant healing or support to a specific person. (Quantum physics is beginning to explain how such grids might work, even across long distances, but you don't need to understand the mechanism to use the effect.) The grid is laid over the name of the person or over a photograph of him or her. Then, placing a combination of healing and clearing crystals ensures that the healing energies gently balance the person's energy field.

Using the grid: This grid should only be used with the permission of the person concerned. If he or she is too ill, or is out of contact, ask that healing be available to him or her for their highest good and benefit—but only if this is appropriate. (If in doubt, dowse, see page 31, to find out whether it is appropriate or not.)

Timing: No specific timing is required. Lay the grid whenever it is needed.

Color and background: Blue is the traditional color of healing.

YOU WILL NEED:

- Sufficient healing and clearing crystals to create the sunburst
- Keystone appropriate to the condition or need

TO LAY THE GRID:

1. Hold the crystals in your hands and state your intention for the grid: namely, that appropriate healing will flow to the person named [insert name] *in the best way possible.*
2. Lay a keystone in the center of the photograph or over the person's name.
3. Lay alternate rows of clearing crystals (pointing outward, if the crystals have points) and rows of healing crystals (pointing inward if the crystals have points).
4. Use the power of your mind to activate the grid. Watch it fire up, clearing and unblocking stuck energies and bringing the person back into balance. (Do not join up the grid—the energy needs to radiate to the person in question.) If the person is ungrounded, you can lay a perimeter of grounding stones, if appropriate. (Dowse, see page 31, or use your intuition to find out whether this is the case.)
5. Leave the grid in place for as long as necessary, or until the issue is resolved. When you're ready to dismantle the grid, follow the instructions on page 39.

Grid-kit suggestions: *Clearing crystals:* Smoky Quartz, Black Tourmaline, Shungite *Healing crystals:* Quantum Quattro, Bloodstone, Que Sera, Amethyst, Quartz, Klinoptilolith, Scolecite with Natrolite, and see page 30.

An Andandalite™ keystone surrounded by a sunburst of Smoky Quartz, Quantum Quattro, Eye of the Storm (Judy's Jasper), and Rose Quartz sent continual healing and support to a dear friend.

ANCESTRAL

**Layout:
Celtic Tree of Life**

The Celtic Tree of Life is the perfect layout for healing the ancestral line and sending healing forward into future generations. It breaks old patterns, switches off detrimental energetic potential in the subtle DNA, and switches on beneficial energetic potential in the DNA, taking the crystal energy deep within the family and between the cells of the physical body.

Using the grid: Use this layout if there has been family and intergenerational trauma or toxic emotions or ingrained patterns carried down through the ancestral line. You can lay it on and around your own body to act as a surrogate for the ancestors and future generations.

Timing: This grid is particularly effective when laid at the dark of the moon and left in place until a full moon. It can also be laid at the winter solstice and can remain in place until the summer solstice, provided it is regularly cleansed and tended as appropriate.

Color and background: A green cloth and/or natural materials, such as wood or stone.

YOU WILL NEED:

- Sufficient crystals for the trunk and base, to represent the present-life family
- Sufficient ancestral or grounding and detoxifying crystals for the roots, to represent the ancestors
- Sufficient light-bringing crystals for the branches, to represent future generations
- Keystone

TO LAY THE GRID:

1. Hold your crystals in your hands and state your intention for the grid.
2. Place appropriate crystals on the trunk to represent the present-life family.
3. Place the ancestral or grounding and detoxifying crystals or anchor stones on the roots.
4. Place the light-bringing crystals in the branches, to represent future generations.
5. Place an anchor stone in the base of the trunk and a keystone above.
6. Use the power of your mind to activate the grid—without connecting it up—and to send healing back into the past and forward into future generations.
7. To dismantle the grid, remove the stones in the reverse order in which they were placed. (There's no need to use sound or clearing essence for dismantling this particular grid. You can happily leave its energy to continue working, even after it's been dismantled.)

NOTE:

If you are laying the Tree on your physical body and the chakras, follow the instructions on page 126.

Grid-kit suggestions: Ancestralite, Brandenberg Amethyst, Cradle of Life (Humankind), Freedom Stone, Kambaba Jasper, Celtic Quartz, Petrified Wood, Preseli Bluestone, Stromatolite, Chrysotile, Dumortierite, Selenite, Petalite, crystals from the ancestral homeland

The ancestral healing grid laid on a purpose-made wooden board. Ancestralite is placed at the base and sides to clear the ancestral line back to its source and bring forward soul learning. Eye of the Storm (Judy's Jasper) stabilizes the Petrified Wood keystone and Smoky Quartz discharges toxic energy into the Flint anchor stones beneath the grid. Selenite and Herkimer Diamonds infuse light into future generations and radiate it back through the family line.

SITUATIONAL

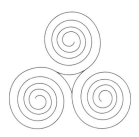

Layout: Triple spiral

The triple spiral layout can be used in a similar fashion to a three-card Tarot spread. It highlights and heals not only the present situation, but also its origins. In this grid, the bottom right-hand spiral represents the present situation; the left-hand spiral reveals and heals the underlying causes behind the situation; and the top spiral ensures a beneficial outcome. It can be used to heal family rifts, in work situations, for friendships, or for the benefit of the wider world.

Using the grid: Use this grid to assist any situation that requires healing and resolution.

Timing: This grid can be laid at any time, but it is particularly potent to lay the right-hand spiral at the dark of the moon; the left-hand one at a new moon; and the top spiral at a full moon. Leave in place until the following dark moon or until the situation has resolved itself.

Color and background: Choose an appropriate color and background for the type of situation involved. Use your intuition, or dowse to decide on color and background.

YOU WILL NEED:

- Template
- Sufficient crystals for each spiral (see grid-kit suggestions below)
- Keystone

TO LAY THE GRID:

1. Hold the crystals for the first spiral in your hands and state your intention for the grid.
2. Lay the right-hand spiral from the center outward. Pointed crystals should be placed point-outward from the center.
3. Use the power of your mind to join up the crystals, moving from the center of the spiral to the center point of the triple spiral.
4. Lay the keystone in the center, restating your intention.
5. Cleanse the grid (but leave it in place, so that you can add spirals during the course of the development of the grid). Lay the second and third spirals in turn as appropriate, connecting to the central keystone each time.
6. Leave the grid in place until the time comes to dismantle it, remembering to cleanse it regularly.

Grid-kit suggestions: *Conflict resolution:* Spirit Quartz, Elestial Quartz, Chalcedony, Chryso-colla, Green Agate, Jade, Picture Jasper, Prehnite, Rose Quartz, Shiva Lingam, Rutilated or Tourminalated Quartz, Strawberry Quartz, Indicolite Quartz, Watermelon Tourmaline
Cleansing: Shungite, Smoky Quartz, Black Tourmaline, Hematite
Light-bringing: Anandalite™, Petalite, Phenacite, Selenite

Spirals of Smoky Quartz, Turquoise, and Amethyst surround a Quartz heart to heal a lack of communication caused by misunderstanding of the core issues and a clash of opposing viewpoints.

ON A MAP

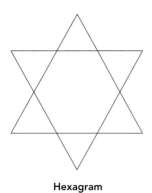

Hexagram

The hexagram layout is extremely stabilizing, so it is particularly appropriate when there has been an upheaval of the earth in a local environment, such as an earthquake or a tsunami. Placed over a map, it facilitates rebalancing and healing the land. Since it is a clearing and transmuting grid, it can also assist in areas where there has been ancestral trauma—such as sites of concentration camps, or other areas where ethnic cleansing has taken place—or land clearing, as in the Amazon rainforests.

Using the grid: Lay the grid where it will not be disturbed, and leave it in place until the situation resolves.

Timing: Use this grid whenever there has been upheaval in the local environment or to assist such a situation anywhere in the world—in which case, place the crystals on a map.

YOU WILL NEED:

- 3 clearing crystals
- 3 earth-healing or light-bringing crystals
- Keystone
- Anchor stones
- Additional crystals as appropriate

TO LAY THE GRID:

1. Hold your crystals in your hands and state your intention for the grid.
2. Lay the upward-pointing triangle with clearing crystals first.
3. Then lay the downward-pointing triangle with healing or light-bringing crystals.
4. Place the keystone in the center and restate your intention.
5. Anchor the grid if appropriate. Dowse (see page 31) or use your intuition to find out whether this is so and which crystals to use.
6. Cleanse the grid regularly and substitute or place additional crystals if appropriate. Leave in place until the situation has been resolved.
7. To dismantle the grid, remove the stones in the reverse order in which they were placed. (There's no need to use sound or clearing essence for dismantling this particular grid. You can happily leave its energy to continue working, even after it's been dismantled.)

Grid-kit suggestions: Anandalite™, Aragonite, Jade, Kiwi Jasper, Magnetite, Smoky Quartz, Rhodozite, Rose Quartz, Quartz, Selenite, Ruby in Kyanite or Zoisite, Smoky Quartz, Hematite, local stones

Following the recurrence of severe earthquakes in the Christchurch area of New Zealand in 2016, a keystone of Pounamou Jade from the local Greenstone trail was laid over the site on a map. An anchoring grid of Rhodozite was laid around it. Kiwi Jasper and Selenite brought in comfort and light to the traumatized inhabitants, and Aragonite sputniks stabilized the equally traumatized land.

GLOSSARY

Arc: A section of the circumference of a circle or a curving trajectory. An arc can also be a sustained luminous discharge of electricity or energy across a gap in a circuit or between electrodes (or crystals).

Astrological elements and triplicities: The zodiac is divided into a series of four equilateral triangles, and each triangle contains the three signs in each element: fire, which represents spirit and creativity; air, which represents inspiration and ideas; earth, which represents pragmatic grounding; and water, which represents emotions and intuition. Within each elemental group, one sign is cardinal; one is fixed; and one is mutable. For example, within the triangle that contains the Earth signs, Taurus is fixed; Virgo is mutable; and Capricorn is cardinal. Cardinal, fixed, and mutable describe how easily and quickly energy and change flow through a sign. "Cardinal" is the initiating energy; "fixed" is the consolidating force; and "mutable" refers to the ability to adapt and go with the flow. So, the first triplicity in the zodiac is fire, in which Aries is cardinal, Leo is fixed, and Sagittarius is mutable.

Axis/Axes: A straight line bisecting—that is, drawn across the center of—a circle and/or through the centers of all circles on a straight line, dividing them in half. It creates symmetrical patterns and reflective space.

Circumference: The outer edge of a circle equidistant from the center.

Diameter: The distance across a circle from edge to edge, passing through the center.

Dis-ease: A state of energetic disharmony created by a discordant environment, toxic emotions, and ingrained thought patterns. Unless it is healed, dis-ease can lead to physical or mental disturbances.

Electromagnetic smog/EMFs: A subtle but detectable electromagnetic field produced by power lines and electrical equipment that has an adverse effect on sensitive people.

Geopathic stress: Negative health effects on the body caused by geoelectromagnetic frequencies and earth energy disturbances. Geopathic stress may be caused by underground water, mining or construction activities, natural or manmade electromagnetic currents, or "dragon" (ley) lines crossing in the vicinity (see *Crystal Prescriptions (Volume 3)* in Resources, page 184).

Grounded: Being grounded means being fully present in incarnation, centered around your core, and solidly anchored in the current moment. It gives a feeling of relaxed certainty and being in control of yourself. You are aware and in touch with the planet, able to function within the practical, everyday world and yet able to extend into spiritual awareness as appropriate.

Hexagram: A six-pointed star or a figure with six equal sides, also known as a hexagon.

Pentagram: A five-pointed star or a figure with five equal sides, also known as a pentagon.

Polygon: A regular-sided figure.

Positive DNA potential: Presently, 97 percent of DNA is identified as "non-functioning," but studies of so-called "junk DNA" show that it contains memories of personal trauma and transgenerational memories, which affect both the karmic blueprint and our subtle energy fields. This has enormous implications for our health, well-being, and evolution. But the good news is that the potential exists to switch off this outdated detrimental genetic coding (including ancestral inheritance) and to switch on beneficial codes to bring about changes in physical, mental, and emotional functioning—like upgrading the random access memory in a computer, having first deconstructed and removed outdated programs and remnants of former programs. (See *Crystal Prescriptions (Volume 6)* in Resources, page 184, for a more in-depth explanation.)

Radius: Half the width of a circle, measured from the center to the outer edge.

Sick-building syndrome: A condition caused by a building with air pollution or inadequate ventilation, excess static electricity, electromagnetic smog, geopathic stress, or related issues. Symptoms include lack of concentration, headache, chest and skin problems, nausea, excessive fatigue, and dizziness.

Ungrounded: Ungroundedness is the opposite of being grounded. When someone is ungrounded, he or she has only a toehold in incarnation, being unattached to the world and everyday reality. He or she is impractical, airheaded, forgetful, inattentive, and disconnected; he or she feels insecure and lacks a sense of control, and probably suffers from hyper-anxiety.

RESOURCES

PUBLICATIONS BY JUDY HALL

101 Power Crystals: The Ultimate Guide to Magical Crystals, Gems, and Stones for Healing and Transformation. Beverly, MA: Fair Winds Press, 2011.

The Crystal Bible (Volumes 1–3). London: Godsfield Press Ltd, 2013.

The Crystal Companion. London: Godsfield Press Ltd, 2017.

The Crystal Experience: Your Complete Crystal Workshop in a Book. London: Godsfield Press Ltd, 2012.

Crystal Prescriptions: The A–Z Guide to over 1,200 Symptoms and Their Healing Crystals. Hampshire, UK: O Books, 2006.

Crystal Prescriptions: The A–Z Guide to over 1,250 Conditions and Their New Generation Healing Crystals (Volume 2). Hampshire, UK: O Books, 2014.

Crystal Prescriptions: Crystal Solutions to Electromagnetic Pollution and Geopathic Stress. An A–Z Guide (Volume 3). Hampshire, UK: O Books, 2015.

Crystal Prescriptions: The A–Z Guide to Chakra and Kundalini Awakening Crystals (Volume 4). Hampshire, UK: O Books, 2015.

Crystal Prescriptions: Space Clearing, Feng Shui and Psychic Protection. An A–Z Guide (Volume 5). Hampshire, UK: O Books, 2016.

Crystal Prescriptions: Crystals for Ancestral Clearing, Soul Retrieval, Spirit Release and Karmic Healing. An A–Z Guide (Volume 6). Hampshire, UK: O Books, 2017.

The Crystal Wisdom Healing Oracle: 50 Crystal Cards for Healing, Self-Understanding and Divination. London: Watkins Publishing, 2016.

Crystals and Sacred Sites: Use Crystals to Access the Power of Sacred Landscapes for Personal and Planetary Transformation. Beverly, MA: Fair Winds Press, 2012.

Earth Blessings: Using Crystals for Personal Energy Clearing, Earth Healing and Environmental Enhancement. London: Watkins Publishing, 2014.

The Encyclopedia of Crystals. Beverly, MA: Fair Winds Press, 2007.

Good Vibrations: Psychic Protection, Energy Enhancement and Space Clearing. Bournemouth, UK: Flying Horse Books, 2008.

Judy Hall's Book of Psychic Development. Bournemouth, UK: Flying Horse Books, 2014.

Life-Changing Crystals: Using Crystals to Manifest Abundance, Wellbeing and Happiness. London: Godsfield Press Ltd, 2013.

Psychic Self-Protection: Using Crystals to Change Your Life. London: Hay House, 2009.

Crystals to Empower You: Use Crystals and the Law of Attraction to Manifest Abundance, Wellbeing and Happiness. London: Godsfield Press Ltd, 2013.

Crystal Love: Attract Your Soul Mate, Improve Your Sex Life, and Much More. London: Godsfield Press Ltd, 2008.

CRYSTAL CLEANSING AND RECHARGING SPRAYS

Crystal Balance, www.crystalbalance.co.uk
Green Man Shop, www.greenmanshop.co.uk
Krystal Love, www.krystallove.com.au
Petaltone Essences (United Kingdom), www.petaltone.co.uk
Petaltone Essences (United States of America), www.petaltoneusa.com
Petaltone Essences (Japan), www.petaltone-jp.com
Spiritual Planet, www.spiritualplanet.co.uk

CRYSTALS

Exquisite Crystals
www.exquisitecrystals.com
John van Rees

Astrologywise
www.astrologywise.co.uk
Judy Hall

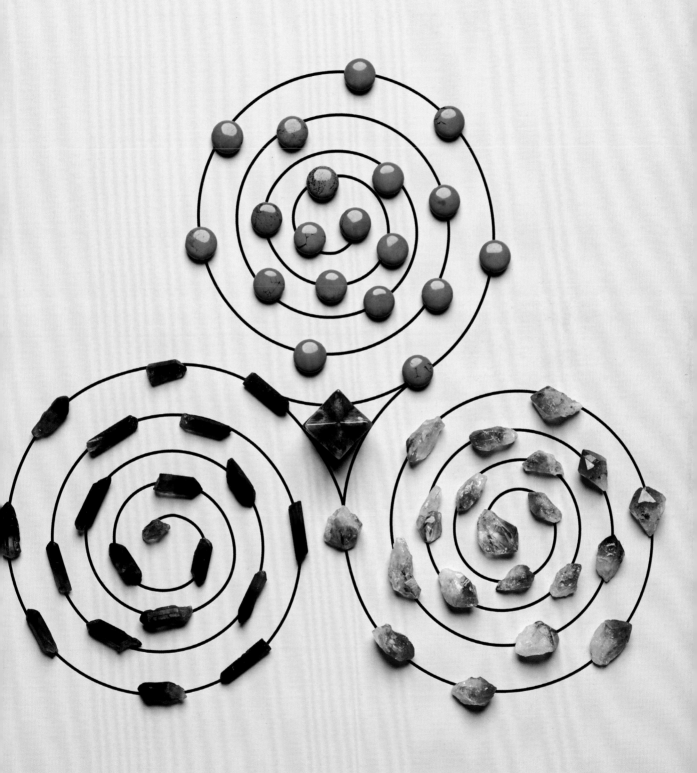

ACKNOWLEDGMENTS

I would like to thank Michael Illas for his skill, care, and sensitivity when photographing the crystals and layouts, and all the workshop participants who have assisted in earth healing and grid work over the years and who have taught me so much. I much appreciated Yulia Surnina's assistance in setting out some of the grids and sorting through my crystal treasure trove. Many thanks go to Megan Buckley.

ABOUT THE AUTHOR

Judy Hall (Dorset, England) is a successful Mind-Body-Spirit author with more than 47 MBS books to her credit including the million copy selling *Crystal Bible* (volumes 1, 2, and 3), *101 Power Crystals*, *Crystals and Sacred Sites*, *Crystal Prescriptions*, and *The Crystal Wisdom Healing Oracle*. A trained healer and counselor, Judy has been psychic all her life and has a wide experience of many systems of divination and natural healing methods. Judy has a B.Ed in Religious Studies with an extensive knowledge of world religions and mythology and an M.A. in Cultural Astronomy and Astrology at Bath Spa University. Her expertise are past life readings and regression; soul healing, reincarnation, astrology and psychology, divination, and crystal lore. Judy has appeared four times in the Watkins list of the 100 most influential spiritual living writers and was voted the 2014 Kindred Spirit MBS personality of the year. An internationally known author, psychic, and healer, Judy conducts workshops in her native England and internationally. Her books have been translated into nineteen languages.

CRYSTAL GRID INDEX

BASIC GRIDS

ADVANCED GRIDS

SPECIFIC GRIDS

PERSONAL

HOME AND ENVIRONMENT

DISTANCE HEALING

EARTH HEALING

INDEX

ALSO BY JUDY HALL

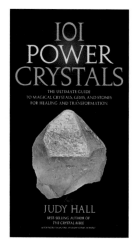

101 POWER CRYSTALS
978-1-59233-490-2

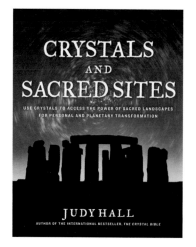

CRYSTALS AND SACRED SITES
978-1-59233-522-0

ENCYCLOPEDIA OF CRYSTALS, REVISED AND EXPANDED
978-1-59233-582-4

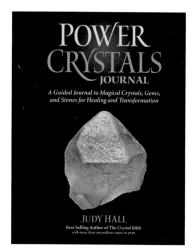

POWER CRYSTALS JOURNAL
978-1-59233-627-2